Business Organisation

Studymates

Many other titles in preparation

Business Organisation

Teresa Holmes

www.**studymates**.co.uk

Copyright 2001 by Teresa Holmes

First published in 2001 by Studymates Limited, PO Box 2, Taunton, Somerset TA3 3YE

Telephone: (01823) 432002
Fax: (01823) 430097

Typeset by PDQ Typesetting, Newcastle-under-Lyme, Staffordshire.
Printed and bound in Great Britain by Bell & Bain Ltd., Glasgow

Contents

Preface

Business Organisation is intended as an introductory guide for students but it is equally applicable to those who work in business and who need to understand the full nature of the organisations within which they work.

This book is also essential reading for ITC professionals and students studying information and communications technology. When there is a need to integrate an ICT system into an organisation, a clear understanding of that organisation is vital for its successful implementation. The aim of the book, therefore, is to present an integrated view of organisations from the inside.

The book stresses the importance of viewing an organisation as a whole – and the importance of searching for links between the design, functions, structures, behaviours, policies and procedures that are found in all types of organisation, regardless of their nature or size.

To assist in this task, you are encouraged to enter an organisation and browse. You must become actively involved in your learning by completing the activities and exercises provided in the tutorials at the end of the chapters. You also need to identify the key points and to apply the concepts and principles presented here to organisations you know.

The book is an essential guide to all who need to understand the nature of organisations. It is concise but comprehensive and explains how you can interact with organisations at different levels. It is carefully formatted, with a framework that covers the key points of organisational behaviour, design and structure.

I hope teachers and lecturers will find the book of benefit and I urge those who do to mention it to others. As a teacher, I want to help you understand these concepts and I want to help you to help others.

Teresa Holmes

Publisher's note

I am delighted to be welcoming Teresa Holmes to this growing Studymates list. She has expertise that can only benefit both students and those in business. Read this book thoroughly and learn from her knowledge. Teresa Holmes writes well and explains difficult concepts very clearly. This is why we are so pleased to welcome her to the team as one of your Studymates Experts.

Graham Lawler MA (AKA the Broadcaster 'Mr Educator'
Studymates Limited

1

Organisations as Systems

One-minute summary – By adopting a systems approach to the study of business organisations, organisations can be studied in the context of their biological, mechanical and social roots. Organisational systems can be either open or closed, simple or complex. Organisations must respond not only to changes within themselves but also to changes in their external environments. This chapter will help you to understand:

▶ a systems approach to studying organisations
▶ systems and subsystems
▶ open versus closed systems
▶ simple versus complex systems
▶ the organisation and its external environment
▶ the usefulness of a systems approach.

A systems approach to studying organisations

An introduction to organisations

Organisations may be described as formalised groups of people engaged in common, goal-directed activities within specified boundaries. They differ in terms of size, purpose, structure, sources of finance, methods of control, adaptability, stage of development and effectiveness.

The study of organisations may be approached from various angles, depending on the discipline involved. Examples of these disciplines are provided below. If your discipline is not included here, spend a few moments considering how a knowledge of organisations may be applicable to your area.

▶ *Business studies* – the structure of different types of

organisation, size differences, ownership, control, regulatory bodies.

▶ *Politics* – political parties, pressure groups, government structures, international bodies, quangos.

▶ *Sociology* – family units, support networks, work groups, communities.

▶ *Psychology* – schools, workplace groups, psychiatric hospitals.

▶ *Law* – firms of solicitors, law courts, industrial tribunals.

Although you will find it useful to analyse organisations from the point of view of particular subject areas, this approach does have its limitations. This is because many organisations have cross-disciplinary functions (such as law courts, schools and business organisations). Also, matching different types of organisations to different disciplines tells us little about the organisations them-selves. To understand organisations more fully, therefore, we need to probe deeper than this.

To begin with, it is useful to take a general overview of organisations before placing any individual organisation under the analytical microscope. This macro approach to studying organisations does not conflict with micro approaches to studying organisations (see below): the two approaches are complementary tools in the difficult task of understanding how organisations function.

An introduction to systems

Viewing organisations as systems may appear daunting at first but it does provide us with an opportunity to impose a structure on to our investigations. A systems approach focuses on a complex set of inter-relationships between different parts of the whole. It enables us to follow the processes involved in maintaining effective operations within an organisation.

The study of the processes found within organisations involves identifying what comes into the system, what happens to these inputs and what they eventually become. For example, in a shoe factory, what raw materials, machinery and staff are required to produce shoes? What stages or processes occur in order to produce shoes? What types of shoes are produced? This principle applies equally well to service industries such as hospitals, schools, insurance companies and travel agents.

Before going any further, it is useful to return to the question of relevance to particular disciplines. In many ways, using a systems approach makes it easier to identify the similarities and differences between subject areas. To try this out, look at the examples given below and broaden these to encompass the wider systems found within your own subject area. If you are involved in more than one discipline, you should find it useful to compare and contrast examples of systems found in your various subject areas:

▶ legal system
▶ political system
▶ social system
▶ biological system
▶ engineering system.

These examples demonstrate a *macro* approach to the study of systems. In other words, they encourage us to take an overview of the *whole* system. Although this provides us with an outline view of a system's constituent parts, it is too broad to provide a detailed understanding of how a particular system works. To achieve this we need to adopt a *micro* perspective and divide a system into smaller parts. For example:

▶ different types of court within the legal system
▶ a political party at national and local levels
▶ methods of communication within a school
▶ the human circulatory system and how it operates
▶ a central heating system and how it operates.

Although for the sake of example the scale of these systems has been greatly reduced, we can still appreciate that the scope of their operations is still quite extensive. Breaking them down further, therefore, should aid our analysis even more. Taking a communications system as an example, this could be further subdivided into different *methods* of communication. These could include voice mail, letters, email, internal and external telephones, memos and notice boards. Each of these divisions may be regarded as a system in its own right. But they are still subdivisions, or subsystems, of the larger system of which they are a part.

Systems and subsystems

Subsystems

If we return to the main theme of looking at organisations as a whole, we should now be aware that organisations comprise varying numbers of subsystems each operating at different levels. This is because most organisations are far too large to operate effectively as *entire* systems. Instead, specific functions are performed by specific parts or areas of the organisation – in other words, by *subsystems*.

Subsystems within organisations differ according to the role they play. For convenience, however, they can be analysed in terms of the general functions they perform. In some organisations, subsystems may be designed to deal with particular functions; in others they may be cross-functional. The terms used to describe these functions vary but, in essence, they may be categorised as follows. Those:

► providing essential links with other subsystems within the organisation by, for example, controlling operations, co-ordinating activities and managing conflict

► providing essential links with other organisations outside their boundaries. Responsibilities would include, for example, obtaining the necessary inputs of supplies and materials and creating markets for outputs

► processing the inputs to provide appropriate outputs. This applies equally to goods or services

► concerned with making sure the organisation runs smoothly in terms of physical maintenance and the care of its human resources

▶ entrusted with ensuring the organisation remains adaptable and flexible in response to pressures to change from both inside and outside its boundaries.

If this approach seems confusing, there are alternative, perhaps simpler, ways of categorising organisational subsystems. One way is to consider the different features found in most organisations which they need in order to operate effectively. These might include:

▶ *strategy* – the organisation's vision and planning
▶ *management* – how an organisation is controlled and directed
▶ *human resources* – the types of people employed and their dominant culture
▶ *structure* – the construction or form an organisation takes
▶ *technology* – the type of machinery and equipment available to transform inputs into outputs.

However we categorise subsystems it should be apparent they are the building blocks of an organisation. To gain a full understanding of the overall system, therefore, we need to peel away the layers until all the subsystems are exposed (Figure 1).

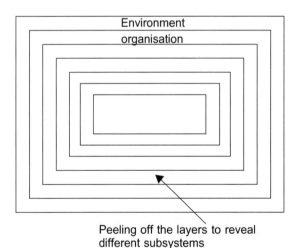

Figure 1. Subsystems: Peeling back the layers.

Not all subsystems have equal importance, and the relative importance of specific subsystems will vary between organisations. Hence subsystems cannot be studied in isolation from other subsystems, from the system as a whole or from the environment. And changes in relative importance can also occur over time.

Open versus closed systems

Closed systems
If an organisation is self-contained, self-sufficient and cut off from the outside world, it is described as a closed system. This means it can function without inputs from its external environment. Closed systems are often described as being 'mechanical' since they are not responsive to what is happening in their environment. Such organisations are inward-looking – concerned with their own designs, structures and procedures.

In principle, stable, predictable systems should be easy to manage. However, because they are so rigid and isolated they are prone to breakdowns and failure. They are also unable to initiate or respond to changes in their environment, which could lead to stagnation and decline (Figure 2). Therefore we can see that, in reality, such extreme forms of closed-system organisations cannot exist.

Open systems
In contrast to closed systems, open systems *do* interact with the outside world. This allows them to influence, as well as be influenced by, their environment, which is essential for their survival. Such systems are likened to biological organisms or dynamic social systems because they can initiate change as well as adapt to changes in their environment.

Open systems are also flexible enough to cope with changes in one or more of their subsystems while keeping the overall system functioning effectively. An open system does this by setting up and maintaining effective communication systems and feedback mechanisms. This is important, as open systems need to anticipate as well as respond to change. If open systems appear complicated this is a result of the diversity of their tasks and also a consequence

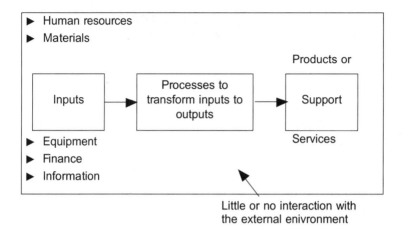

Figure 2. Closed systems.

of the problems they constantly need to resolve. Dependence on their environment also makes them more vulnerable to external influences (Figure 3).

While most systems are open, some subsystems within an organisation may be closed. This could apply to sections or departments that service only other parts of the system. The organisation itself, however, would still need to maintain links with other organisations (for example, it would still need to purchase supplies and sell its products). It would still also be subject to external legal and political controls.

Simple versus complex systems

As we have seen, systems and subsystems vary in their level of complexity. They can also be divided into three main categories: biological, mechanical and social.

Biological systems
These are living, self-maintaining systems, and examples can be found in plants, animals and human beings. They are char-

External environment

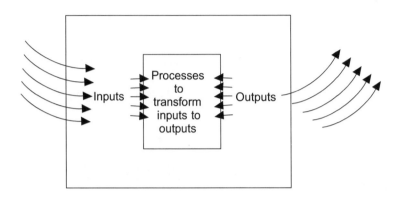

Figure 3. Open systems.

acterised by their ability to interact with their environments and to adapt to changes in that environment in order to survive or to operate more effectively.

Mechanical systems
This category refers to machine systems. Examples include assembly lines in factories, central heating systems and alarm systems. These are characterised by their ability to exert control over their constituent parts and to be self-regulating.

Social systems
This type of system is found only among human beings. Examples include schools, local authorities and nations. They are characterised by a group culture, norms and values. The people who belong to social systems play a specific role or roles that may change over time and with circumstances. Interaction takes place within and between social systems through some form of structured communication.

Mechanical systems are the simplest, followed by biological systems and with social systems the most complex. Organisations generally comprise aspects of all three types of system. Mechanical systems operate to maintain a healthy, safe and secure environment. In some organisations they also produce the goods that are essential for the company's survival. Biological systems could be seen as operating within the human resources function of a company and within any animal or plant life an organisation may have (e.g. a farm or market garden). The organisation as a whole is a social system and contains other, smaller, social systems.

Within each of these systems there are usually a number of subsystems. Mechanical systems may comprise a series of components clustered to form subsystems. A good example of this is a production line in a factory. Deficiencies or breakdowns may result in reduced efficiency or failure of the system as a whole. Biological systems also comprise numerous subsystems. Malfunctions within one of these could have adverse effects on the entire organisation. For example, an individual or team operating at reduced efficiency (for whatever reason) will have repercussions for the organisation as a whole.

Social subsystems within an organisation include teams, sections, departments, branches or even companies. Each subsystem may have its own rules, norms, values and cultures. This can be further complicated in the case of multinational organisations, which often operate across national boundaries.

Managing systems

For an organisation to run smoothly, managers need to be aware of the different types of systems and subsystems under their control. In particular, they need to acknowledge their organisation is a *social* system. As such, it is constantly changing as people enter and leave the organisation. In addition, their organisation continuously interacts with other organisations within the wider social system. This will lessen the managers' overall control whilst increasing the problems they are likely to face (for example, suppliers may increase prices, banks may increase their rate of interest or governments may introduce more restrictive employment legislation) (Figure 4).

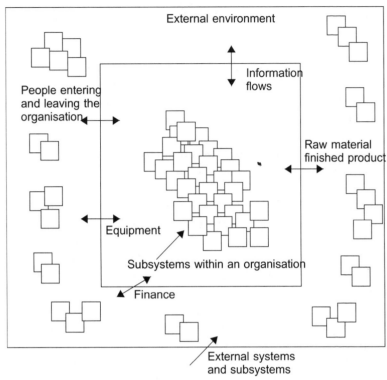

Figure 4. Managing systems.

Controlling systems

This will be discussed in more detail in subsequent chapters. Here, however, we need to look at the design, structure and procedural and psychological aspects of organisations in a broader sense.

Some level of control is essential to make sure organisations operate effectively. The methods chosen will reflect the organisation's legal composition, functions, purpose, size and culture. In many instances the control mechanisms adopted will be the same throughout the entire organisation. However, in some cases differences will occur, reflecting differences within the system itself. Examples of this include departments, divisions or companies within an organisation that have their own rules and regulations. These variations are usually linked to historical, functional or operational differences between the subsystems concerned.

The organisation and its external environment

As we have seen, organisations are open systems, which means their control mechanisms are affected by changes occurring in the outside environment. These changes include economic, legal, political, social and technological factors. The following examples may help to illustrate this point:

▶ *economic* – changes in the rates of interest, inflation, unemployment, taxation

▶ *legal* – changes in statutory requirements relating to employer liability, equal opportunities in the workplace, health and safety regulations

▶ *political* – a change of political party in control of local authorities or central government, the impact of pressure groups, membership of international bodies

▶ *social* – demographic changes, fashion trends, standards of education

▶ *technological* – advances in information technology, scientific and medical developments.

The usefulness of a systems approach

By now you should be aware that adopting a systems perspective encourages people to view organisations as dynamic entities. Much of what we learn about organisations appears contradictory at first but becomes more logical as their story unfolds. Organisations come into existence, develop and grow. Alternatively, if neglected, they can decline and die. They need to be self-regulatory yet are subject to external controls. They seek autonomy whilst recognising the need to interact with their environment. They can be analysed in their entirety or broken down into their constituent parts.

A systems approach to the study of organisations is useful in its own right. It can also form part of a more integrated approach incorporating different perspectives. Organisations can be studied within their historical context, their present position and their likely future roles. Like any organism, an organisation needs to anticipate and embrace change to enhance its chances of survival. Subsystems need to be constantly monitored and maintained to reduce the danger of breakdowns.

Despite the usefulness of a systems approach, it has serious limitations if employed in isolation. You should find that the multiple perspectives adopted here are more fruitful.

Tutorial

Progress questions
1. What is the key difference between an open and closed system?

2. (a) Give three examples of subsystems within an organisation that produces cars. (b) Identify a potential threat to one of these subsystems and suggest ways to minimise that threat.

3. Explain how an organisation could initiate change within the larger system of which it is a part.

Seminar discussion
1. How can a system be both open and closed?

2. Consider how your own discipline can be analysed using a systems perspective.

Practical assignment
Select one organisation and analyse it using a systems perspective. Identify any threats you discover this organisation may face from its environment and suggest ways to minimise these threats.

Study, revision and exam tips
1. Identify key points that require further explanation and undertake additional reading on these.

2. Refer to the glossary whenever you are unclear about the meaning of a word or phrase.

Organisational Structure and Design

One-minute summary – The structure an organisation adopts provides the framework within which it pursues its operations. Over the years the original design may become disjointed and fragmented as structural features are changed and added to. This can produce a lack of cohesion that proves detrimental to the effective working of the organisation. This chapter will help you to understand:

▶ the elements of organisational structure
▶ typical examples of organisational structure
▶ the determinants (causes) of organisational structure
▶ design aspects of organisations
▶ organisational life-cycles.

The elements of organisational structure

An introduction to organisational structure

Structure helps to organise what would otherwise be fragmented components into a cohesive whole. 'Structure' is easy to recognise if we look at a car, bridge or building. When looking at organisations, however, this structure may be less apparent but it is just as important.

Organisational structure refers to the formal patterns of interactions and co-ordination that enable an organisation to achieve its goals. This involves linking the tasks of individuals and groups within the organisation together to enable them to work with one another most effectively.

To understand an organisation's structure, it is useful to view the organisation as a series of stages. Together these allow a product to be made or service to be offered. An example of this might be as follows:

1. identify the tasks needed to produce the product or service

2. allocate these tasks to individual job roles

3. cluster job roles into groups

4. allocate leaders to these groups

5. define how these groups relate to each other

6. draw up a list of procedures, rules and regulations to govern how individuals and groups work together

7. devise a way of showing responsibilities and accountability between individuals and groups.

Although in a simplified form, this example shows how an organisational structure could be designed and developed into a working system. To standardise the classification of systems between organisations, these components are usually identified according to their job title or section or departmental name. The links between them then become lines of authority between different levels of the organisation and lines of co-ordination between teams and departments. The best way to represent these is by the use of an organisation chart.

The organisation chart

A good way to study structure is through an organisation chart. This is a representation of the whole set of underlying activities and processes within an organisation (Figure 5). Organisation charts thus play an important part in helping people to identify the main components of an organisation's structure.

The purpose of this structure is to:

1. define formal relationships (such as the number of levels in the hierarchy and the range of control of managers and supervisors)

2. identify how individuals are grouped into departments and departments into the total organisation

3. help design systems that allow effective communication, co-ordination and integration between departments.

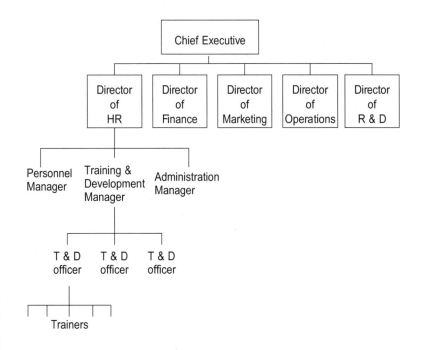

Figure 5. Simple organisation chart.

These three elements of structure apply to both the vertical (lines of authority) and horizontal (at the same level) components of an organisation. (If you are not sure about this, refer back to the organisation chart.) Vertical structure and formal authority are generally stronger than horizontal relationships. However, to work efficiently, an organisation's structure needs to achieve the correct balance between the two.

As you can see from Figure 5, an organisation chart is made up of lines and boxes. This reflects what is happening (or should be happening) within an organisation. Its purpose is to show the activities, employees and co-ordination processes that enable the organisation to achieve its goals. The role of managers is to implement what is shown on the chart to make sure the organisation does in fact achieve its goals.

Typical examples of organisational structure

To help us understand the nature and form of organisational structures, it is best to look at a few examples. One way of doing this is to consider actual companies and the structures they have adopted. However, an alternative, more useful way is to consider some of the typical structures used by organisations.

Simple structure
This structure is most common among new or small organisations. Usually, the manager at the top of the structure has control over all or most areas of the business. In such organisations it is common for all employees to report directly to the top manager. Managers or supervisors would co-ordinate their own areas of responsibility but these people, too, would be directly responsible to the top manager. In these organisations there are few formal policies and procedures: all goals and decisions stem from the top and employees have little authority or scope for initiative.

Complex structure
In this context, complexity can refer to either the number of levels within an organisation (vertical complexity), or the number of departments or jobs (horizontal complexity).

A complex structure is most common in large organisations, where it is linked to decision-making processes: large organisations tend to delegate various types of authority to managers at different levels. Organisations where decisions are made at the top level are described as *centralised*. In *decentralised* organisations, on the other hand, decisions are made at a lower level.

Bureaucracy
As organisations increase in size, their procedures and structures usually become more formal. Such organisations are often referred to as bureaucratic. Bureaucratic is also sometimes used to describe companies that are too rigid. Bureaucracies usually have the following characteristics:

▶ strict rules and regulations
▶ clearly specified functions

- ▶ strict division of labour with roles/duties clearly stated
- ▶ a hierarchy – a chain of command structure where everyone is responsible to someone at a higher level.

Organic

Organic organisations tend to be flexible: they adapt and respond efficiently and effectively to new demands. The key features of organic structures are as follows:

- ▶ people are valued for their knowledge and abilities rather than for their jobs or status

- ▶ problem-solving is left to the most appropriate people

- ▶ status and expertise are not necessarily related

- ▶ decision-making is decentralised. This provides opportunities for people to voice their opinions

- ▶ communication flows freely between different levels, teams and task forces. This means expertise and information are shared across diverse areas.

Bases of authority

All organisations must have some recognisable and acceptable source of authority. Three common forms of authority are as follows:

1. *legal-rational* – employees accept that those with authority have the right to give orders. Rules are accepted as being legal

2. *traditional* – certain posts are traditionally accepted as carrying authority

3. *charismatic* – authority is linked to particular, charismatic individuals.

The determinants (causes) of organisational structure

Organisations need to select a structure that is most appropriate to them at a particular point in time. There are a number of key factors that determine this choice.

An organisation's internal environment

This relates to an organisation's decision-making process, which can be subdivided into three components:

1. *Human Resources*, which is responsible for the selection and socialisation of employees; the development of their job-related and interpersonal skills; and their commitment to the organisation's goals and objectives.

2. *Departmental structure*, which determines the degree of interdependence between staff at various levels. It also has to deal with any conflict that arises between staff at these levels.

3. *Goal attainment devices* that try to make sure employees at various levels reach the goals they are set.

External organisational environments

These are generally classified into four groups along two dimensions:

1. the simple–complex dimension takes account of the different environments in which the organisation must function

2. the stable–dynamic dimension is concerned with the environmental changes an organisation must face.

(The environment an organisation operates within is covered in more detail in later chapters.)

Technology

Technology refers to transformation process – the way an organisation changes its inputs into outputs. For example, if we take all the ingredients needed to make a car, how are these used to produce the vehicles that roll off production lines? Technology, however, is too important to be dealt with in a short paragraph. You will find more detailed coverage in the next chapter.

Life-cycle

Just as all products and services are thought to have life-cycles, so too do organisations. The stage they have reached in this cycle will influence their structure. Generally, structures become more formal the older organisations get. Structure is also influenced by the events that occurred at the time an organisation was formed.

Size

This can be measured in a variety of ways. For example:

▶ the amount of sales
▶ the size of capital investment
▶ the size of the organisation's budget
▶ the number of employees.

Generally speaking, the larger an organisation the more formal its structure, the more specialised are its tasks, and more people are employed in an administrative capacity.

Design aspects of organisations

When designing an effective structure for an organisation, a number of points need to be considered:

▶ the organisation's purpose, size, legal identity and future plans

▶ the tasks of particular employees and how these tasks will be grouped

▶ how the functions and sections of the organisation are inter-related

▶ the flow of work between sections and departments

▶ the degree of standardisation of procedures between departments

▶ the processes involved in producing a good or service

▶ the extent to which the input of one section is the output of another

▶ the need for frequent and effective communication between departments.

Some basic structures are suitable for most types of organisation. However, there are specific structures that are best suited to particular types of organisation (e.g. manufacturing or service industries, or large or small organisations).

A key question to ask at the design stage is whether you need a functional structure or a product structure for your organisation.

Functional structures

In functional structures, activities and people are grouped together by common functions at all levels of the organisation. Each functional department provides resources (for example, engineering, marketing, research and development) to the organisation's overall production process.

Functional structures work best when an organisation places a great deal of emphasis on efficiency, quality and specialisation. Each department then sets its own goals, values and orientations. This usually results in strong departmental allegiance. Consequently, co-operation and co-ordination with other departments can be difficult.

This type of structure works best in the following conditions:

▶ when the external environment is stable

▶ when the organisation has routine technology

▶ when there is a high level of internal efficiency

▶ where only a few products (or services) are involved

▶ when the business is small enough to be controlled and co-ordinated mainly through a vertical hierarchy

▶ where each function plans and manages its own budget which reflects the cost of the resources as used by that department.

A functional structure has the advantage of promoting economy of scale within functions. It also allows staff to specialise and to develop their skills more fully than in other forms of structure. On the other hand, a functionally divided organisation does have a number of weaknesses:

▶ it may respond slowly to environmental changes
▶ decision bottlenecks are likely to occur
▶ there may be poor co-ordination between departments
▶ a lack of innovation
▶ a restricted view of organisational goals.

Product structures
This refers to a divisional structure or a collection of self-contained units. Divisions can be organised in a number of different ways. For example, along the lines of:

▶ individual products
▶ groups of products
▶ services offered
▶ regions
▶ markets
▶ customers
▶ major operational programmes.

However they are grouped, the division is based on organisational outputs. Each grouping or unit is smaller than in a functional structure. This makes them flexible and responsive to the changing needs of their environment. Decisions tend to be decentralised since lines of authority stem from a lower level in the hierarchy. This makes it easy to co-ordinate the work of different departments.

   A product structure is popular with large companies. The smaller units (based on different products) are easy to control and co-ordinate. Medium-sized companies may adopt a similar structure, although the separate units will be smaller.

   The main advantages of a product structure are:

▶ staff can identify with their product unit

▶ units can be run as separate businesses

▶ they are suited to fast change in unstable environments

▶ client satisfaction tends to be high due to clear product responsibility and contact points

▶ there is a high level of co-ordination across functions

▶ units can adapt to differences in products, regions or clients.

The weaknesses of a product structure include:

▶ it cannot take advantage of the economies of scale as in functional departments

▶ it can lead to poor co-ordination across product lines

▶ it eliminates in-depth competence and technical specialisation

▶ it can be difficult to integrate and standardise this structure across product lines.

Vertical structures
A vertical structure will pose, and give answers to, the following types of question:

▶ Who does what within the organisation?

▶ Who reports to whom?

▶ What are the chains of command?

▶ What are the departmental groupings within the organisation?

▶ What are the links between different departments?

▶ How do departments communicate with each other?

Both functional and product structures usually need some form of vertical structure.

Horizontal structures

This type of structure is also important to all organisations and, again, can be clearly identified on an organisation chart. The main purpose of a horizontal structure is to:

▶ overcome communication barriers between departments
▶ provide opportunities for co-ordination among employees
▶ unify efforts to achieve organisational objectives.

How this is achieved and the mechanisms used will vary with:

▶ the size and type of organisation
▶ its geographical spread
▶ its current state of technology.

Liaising with different departments is essential within horizontal structures. Once again, how this is done will vary between different types of organisation.

Matrix structures

This form allows functional and product structures to be used together. In a matrix system, functional and product managers have equal authority over the employees. A matrix structure is most likely to operate when:

1. An organisation needs resources across its product lines. This usually occurs in medium-sized companies with a moderate range of products. A matrix structure permits the flexible use of people and equipment to meet company needs.

2. There is pressure from the environment that can only be met by operating along functional and product lines (for example, if there is a demand for a high technical quality or the frequent launch of new products).

3. Externally, an organisation has to operate within a complex and uncertain environment. Internally, there will be a high degree of interdependence between departments. This will require effective co-ordination and information processing in both the vertical and horizontal directions.

The main advantages of a matrix system include:

- ▶ effective co-ordination between departments
- ▶ high flexibility due to the sharing of people and resources
- ▶ opportunities for the development of function and product skills.

The main disadvantages of a matrix system include:

- ▶ the danger of conflict between managers of equal status

- ▶ employees being placed in a difficult position as managers compete for their time

- ▶ time can be wasted trying to resolve difficulties that arise through dual authority

- ▶ it may be difficult to reach decisions

- ▶ dual pressure from the environment is required to maintain the balance of power between conflicting authorities.

To try to resolve the difficulties created by a matrix system it is necessary to:

- ▶ employ people with high levels of interpersonal skills

- ▶ provide extensive training for managers and employees

- ▶ set up appropriate mechanisms to speed up decision-making and to resolve conflict.

Hybrid structures

Hybrid refers to any structure that is not 'pure'. In reality, most organisations contain elements of different types of structures. This gives them the opportunity to take advantage of the strengths of all the different types. However, there is the danger organisations will inherit the structures' weaknesses as well. Most organisations, however, find that some hybrid structure is the best way of achieving their goals.

It is tempting to view organisational design as something that occurs at the start of a company's life-cycle and then just continues. This is unlikely, however, since organisational needs are constantly changing. The original designs then become inadequate or inappropriate.

An organisation's current structure often bears little resemblance to its original design: changes will have taken place gradually and piecemeal. While this situation is far from ideal, it is based on the need to survive and prosper. As a result, it may be difficult to identify clearly a particular structure from the hybrid it has become.

Organisational structure also tends to change as companies grow. Generally they grow because:

▶ growth is a company goal

▶ they want to attract top executives who like the challenge/ opportunities provided

▶ of financial reasons (for example, economies of scale can reduce costs).

Design changes due to structural deficiency
Each of the structural forms we have outlined – functional, product, matrix and hybrid – is designed to maximise organisational efficiency. To maintain this, structures need to be evaluated regularly. If deficiencies are found, change must result. Symptoms of structural deficiencies include:

1. *Slow or poor quality decision-making.* This may be due to a number of factors, such as work overload, insufficient delegation to lower levels, poor communications and ineffective co-ordination.

2. *Reduced innovation in response to a changing environment.* This may be due to poor horizontal co-ordination within departments, inadequate knowledge of consumer needs and inadequate technological development.

3. *Excessive conflict between departmental and organisational goals.* A likely explanation is inadequate horizontal links.

Organisational life-cycles

As we saw earlier in this chapter, organisations go through a series of stages that are related to their position in the organisational life-cycle. Typically, these stages are as follows.

The entrepreneurial stage
The initial stage when a new product or service is created. The most important goal is survival. Companies at this stage are usually small and non-bureaucratic. Control and supervision tend to be informal and rest with the owner-entrepreneur. Long hours are often worked to develop, produce and sell the new product or service. If the company succeeds, it employs more staff and delegates planning to professional managers.

The collectivity stage
At this stage employees (usually) strongly identify with the company and work hard to make it succeed. This is a youthful stage of rapid growth and enthusiasm. Key concerns at this stage are human resource issues, such as:

▶ co-operation
▶ maintaining employee commitment
▶ morale
▶ personalised leadership.

As the organisation progresses through this stage, more formal systems develop: structured departments, job assignments and a hierarchy of authority all emerge. Workers and lower-level managers may feel more isolated from the major decisions made by senior managers. Problems of delegation and control may occur. To help resolve these problems, the organisation must develop a formal system of delegation.

The formalisation stage
In organisational terms, the company is in middle age. It has expanded and probably needs to employ more specialist staff. It has also become more bureaucratic. Information and control systems are needed to combat communication problems. There is

an increasing emphasis on measuring effectiveness, reaching specified goals and increasing productivity. Towards the end of this stage, the organisation appears too large to operate effectively.

The elaboration stage
By now the organisation is large and bureaucratic with extensive systems, rules and regulations. It recognises the need to develop ways for employees to work together effectively. The emphasis shifts away from bureaucracy towards a renewed interest in co-operation and teamwork. Decentralisation is used to help balance the conflicting demands for differentiation and integration. Social control and self-discipline are encouraged to reduce the need for more formal procedures.

Maintaining and enhancing the company's reputation and status become key goals. Creativity and innovation are again valued. Formal systems are simplified and alternative methods of communication and control are sought, such as project teams or task forces.

The organisation devotes more energy to monitoring its product cycles. It becomes more responsive to changes in the environment and in technology. Outsiders may be recruited to senior positions to revitalise the organisation and to move it forward.

Tutorial

Progress questions
1. What is the main difference between a functional and a product structure?

2. What is the main difference between a vertical and horizontal structure?

3. Why is it important to understand the life-cycle of an organisation?

Practical assignment
Investigate an organisation of your choice to identify:

► its stage in the organisational life-cycle
► the main structure it has adopted
► why it chose that particular structure.

Draw an organisation chart for either the whole organisation or a single department. Use the chart to help you understand its organisational structure more fully.

Study, revision and exam tips

1. Practise drawing and adapting organisation charts.

2. Link the theoretical points outlined in this chapter to actual organisations.

Technological and Environmental Issues

One-minute summary – Technology has always played a major role in the success of organisations. With today's emphasis on rapid change, it is even more essential a company has the technology it needs to remain competitive. However, this must be weighed against the implications of advanced technology for human resources and for the wider environment in general. This chapter will help you to understand:

▶ the nature of technology within organisations
▶ the impact of technology on human resources
▶ technology and change
▶ the external environment
▶ environmental issues.

The nature of technology within organisations

The meaning of technology
Technology refers to the various means available to an organisation to transform its inputs into outputs. In simple terms, technology is what people use to get things done. It includes formulae, equipment and machinery. Technology has become increasingly important because of its recent rapid advances. Advances in technology are supposed to make production easier and quicker but, as you will discover, this is not always the case.

Leading-edge technology
The phrase 'leading edge' has become commonplace in relation to design and technology. Some organisations think they only have to purchase the latest technology to sprint ahead of their rivals. Even if this works, any advantage is likely to be temporary as competitors catch up and then overtake them.

Organisations differ in the extent to which they need certain types of technology. This is related to such factors as:

▶ the size of the organisation
▶ its product or service
▶ its position in the marketplace
▶ its organisational structure
▶ the technology currently available in its field of work.

Some technology is now so widely used it is difficult to imagine any organisation being without it. Computers are an obvious example. However, even here differences occur. Some organisations need basic skills and equipment only. Others require the most advanced software and hardware available.

Mass-produced versus customised products

This is a major factor in deciding what type of technology to use. If an organisation mass produces standardised products, access to advanced technology is important. This should speed up production and reduce costs.

Organisations that supply a relatively customised product or a personal service may not need such advanced technology. A compromise would be to supply fairly standard products retailers or customers can then personalise themselves. Examples of this would include the fast-food industry and the provision of components for self-assembly.

When deciding which technology to employ, organisations need to consider their own specific needs:

▶ How standardised are their products?

▶ How many products are manufactured per day, week, month or year?

▶ What degree of flexibility do they need from their technology?

▶ How often will they need to change their technology?

▶ What type of technology is used by their competitors and to what effect?

▶ How easily can their existing technology be upgraded and at what cost?

The impact of technology on human resources

Benefits versus threats of new technology

The impact of advanced technology on those people who will use it should always be taken into consideration, and the debate about this can be quite heated. To arrive at a satisfactory outcome it is important to consider the benefits and threats of new technology for a company's workforce.

The benefits of new technology for the workforce are often cited as:

▶ reduced physical effort required to perform tasks
▶ improved communication systems
▶ greater flexibility in terms of how and where they work
▶ a more pleasant and healthier environment in which to work.

To some extent the benefits listed here are real. However, they relate mainly to those workers who have survived the introduction of technology. These are usually the more highly skilled professional and technical workers and their position may indeed be enhanced by advances in technology, although this does not always happen.

The disadvantages of introducing new technology include:

▶ a reduction in low-skilled clerical and manual jobs

▶ all work can become more routine and boring

▶ there is less scope for the use of initiative even by highly skilled workers

▶ people generally feel threatened by new technology

▶ difficulty in coping with rapid change and complex new systems

▶ a reduction in skill levels.

Workers' fear of new technology, however, does appear to be justified. Where it has been introduced, trends show a dramatic decrease in low-skill jobs. This reflects the degree of technological knowledge now required from workers involved in mechanised or automated systems.

High labour costs and inflexible working practices have encouraged organisations to consider non-human labour. This is particularly true in countries such as the USA and western Europe that face strong competition from emerging economies.

Both manufacturing and service sectors have changed to more automated systems. The advantages of replacing human resources with non-human labour include the following. Non-human labour will:

▶ work long hours without breaks
▶ work shifts without overtime
▶ not go on strike
▶ not need to engage in social interaction during working hours
▶ be punctual and reliable and will not take time off.

Integrating human and automated systems

Some organisations (for example, in manufacturing) have introduced robots to work alongside the workers. Once again, the impact on the workforce needs to be considered.

Robots are generally defined as machines that can sense, think and act in repeatable cycles. So far their impact on the labour-force, structure, functioning or effectiveness of an organisation is difficult to assess. Feedback from employees who work alongside robots indicates that, although they have little need for higher levels of technical knowledge, they are in fact required so to have. It is also quite daunting to be responsible for such expensive equipment. On the social side, they report fewer opportunities to talk to colleagues or customers. This can make the work less enjoyable.

For automated systems to work, it is essential organisations achieve the right balance between people and machines. This usually means redesigning jobs. Employees also need to be convinced that robots are complementary and not potential replacements. Organisations, therefore, need to prevent:

► workers feeling isolated and alienated
► jobs linked to automated tasks becoming too boring
► workers becoming mere monitors of machines
► workers becoming less competent.

If these problems are not resolved, low productivity and poor-quality products are likely to result. This, in turn, may result in further automation if senior managers do not understand the complexities of the situation.

Increased automation need not necessarily result in more routine tasks and boredom. Automation could be used purely for simple tasks, which would change the nature of the jobs and skills required. This should result in a better skilled and trained workforce.

If automation is introduced, its full implications should be considered. Change should be gradual to lessen the impact, and workers should be consulted from the design stage. This should reduce problems or least make them easier to anticipate.

Coping with technological advances

Advances in technology will result in some job losses. Most of these will be low-skilled jobs while the skill level of the remaining jobs may decrease. The most likely casualties are jobs in small to medium-sized companies. These have the greatest need to reduce labour costs and to increase productivity to allow them to compete with larger companies.

Many of the workers under threat from technology belong to trade unions. Unions have adopted two approaches to automation:

1. *Protectionism* – such as attempting to obtain changes in labour contracts to protect employees and to prevent wages being lowered.

2. *Forward-looking strategies* – such as persuading companies to hold regular briefings with workers confronted with technological

advances and helping their members to retrain. Ironically, advanced technology can help workers to retrain at their own pace and convenience (e.g. computer-based learning). This can be a great help to people not used to education and who are apprehensive about traditional classroom-based learning. Companies can fund this type of training. The government, unions and individuals can also make contributions.

Companies benefit from a well-trained workforce. It will also help them to maintain good labour relations. Short-term contracts and temporary labour can be used to compensate for shortfalls while the workers retrain. Flexible working, job sharing, part-time working and working from home are all ways of making use of technology, cutting costs and maintaining a flexible labour option.

Technological changes also affect career structures within organisations. This results from a change in the nature of jobs. Structural changes also reduce opportunities for promotion. On the positive side, advances in technology do create new jobs and careers.

To cope with technological advances, employees and employers should work together. Earlier warnings about changing job- and career- markets should make the transition to using new technology easier. Schools, colleges and universities all have an important role to play here. They can encourage students to accept and to work with the new technology. They can also offer appropriate courses to help students find work in expanding areas.

Advances in technology also change how we work (for example, the great increase in professionals and top executives who now work from home). The spreading use of computer links, faxes, video conferencing and mobile telephones has helped to make the 'office' more mobile. Advantages of such innovations include:

▶ reduced travelling time
▶ saving money on travel expenses
▶ a reduced need for office space.

Against these benefits we must consider the drawbacks. These include:

▶ reduced social interaction
▶ increased feelings of isolation
▶ the need to self-motivate and to manage your time effectively
▶ the need to set your own goals and to work towards these
▶ the need for office equipment in the home
▶ the need for mobile office equipment.

Not everyone will benefit from these more flexible working arrangements. Even workers with the necessary skills may prefer the more conventional office environment. Unfortunately, however, office layouts considered appropriate for new technology reduce the opportunity for social interaction. Hence, this too can result in feelings of isolation, alienation and reduced job satisfaction.

'Gold-collar workers' is the phrase used to describe people with high-level business management and technological skills. These skills must also include an understanding of how to get people and machines to work in harmony.

What is the impact of new technology on consumers? Mass production has brought more products within their price range. However, it has also increased standardisation and reduced the individuality and life span of products. How consumers feel about such changes should not be ignored.

Technology and change

The rate of technological change has increased greatly overall but varies between particular industries. The most rapid changes have occurred in industries where organisations need to keep ahead of their rivals. However, the advantages gained tend to be short-lived, with companies continually scrambling to maintain their position in the marketplace.

Pleasing the consumer

Customer expectations and desires play a major role in this battle for pole position. Customers' insatiable drive for new products and services puts pressure on companies to provide these. In addition to new lines, existing goods are adapted to appear sufficiently different in order to maintain or increase sales. To achieve this goal, organisations need to:

▶ keep tuned in to consumer demands
▶ have the technology to respond to changing consumer demands
▶ have flexible and responsive decision-making processes.

Technological innovations

Advances in technology have increased the speed at which machinery, equipment and labour skills become obsolete. The more a company relies on technology, the greater the danger of this happening.

In some industries, automation has been introduced to increase productivity and to cut costs. In simple terms, this means automation is used to replace people with machines. Examples vary from automated production lines, to cash dispensers, to photographic kiosks, to drinks machines. Two levels of automation can be identified: mechanisation and computer-integrated manufacturing (CIM).

Mechanisation
In a mechanised workplace, machines are programmed to replace people. Generally, machines are faster, more accurate and more consistent. A degree of mechanisation has existed since the start of the industrial revolution. Today, the pace of mechanisation is much faster, and computer chips have enabled new heights of sophistication to be reached. In some industries, robots can perform even complex tasks and have completely replaced people. An example of this is the motor car industry.

CIM
CIM (computer-integrated manufacturing) enables factories to operate with few or no workers. CIM relies on creating links with other computerised systems such as computer-aided design, computer-aided manufacturing and flexible manufacturing. CIM combines task mechanisation with computerised informa-

tion processing about the task. This allows a flexibility not available in unthinking mechanised systems. CIM enables machines to produce efficiently while providing opportunities for the customisation of products to meet customers' specific requirements.

A further technological advance is the introduction of *expert systems*. These are a result of advances in artificial intelligence. Computer programs mimic the thought processes of human experts. For example, through a series of questions they can diagnose faults and recommend solutions to problems. To be useful, these programs need to be accessible to all computer users and should not be too complicated. The main advantages of expert systems include:

► their judgements are quicker and more consistent than human ones

► they can be programmed to be self-correcting or self-generating.

Despite the potential benefits, expert systems should be treated with caution:

► they are only as good as their creators

► to be useful, information needs to be updated continuously

► all their input must be accurate and valid

► people must be prepared to question their judgements and not view them as infallible.

Improved information-processing systems have revolutionised the way data is collected, stored, retrieved and transmitted. Many companies now have electronic record-keeping systems. These include computers, digital scanners, optical character recognisers, laser printers and optical disc storage for the filing and retrieval of original documents. Original documents can include microfilm, sketches, bills, invoices, photographs, etc.

In theory, the main benefits of electronic filing are the

elimination of bulky paper files and their subsequent retrieval through fast key-word searches. Portable computers allow instant access to information wherever it is needed. Technological advances have also greatly speeded up the transmission of information (for example, by faxes, email and mobile telephones).

Information systems can be programmed to collect and compile data automatically. Their performance can be constantly monitored and instant feedback provided to employees. Allowing employees direct access to such information should lessen their fears about the new systems and make the systems appear less threatening.

Technology and quality

Quality has proved to be a problem with mechanised systems as a result of:

▶ high expectations about quality

▶ the high cost of converting plants to mechanised and automated systems

▶ the difficulties of getting a traditional workforce to operate the new automated systems effectively

▶ inadequate appreciation of the difference between mechanisation and intelligent mechanisation

▶ the high output needed if companies are to operate effectively in terms of both production and cost.

The external environment

The major forces outside an organisation can play a crucial role in the organisation's success. As we saw in Chapter 1, organisations are generally open systems: they continually interact with and receive feedback from their external environment. Managers need to be aware of this. They need to understand and monitor continuously the external environments in which they operate.

Types of environment

The more an organisation knows about its external environment the greater its chances of success. Investigations should reveal:

▶ the nature of environmental demands and how these affect the organisation

▶ successful strategies to manage those demands.

Chapter 1 showed it is virtually impossible for organisations to be completely isolated from environmental influences. However, it is difficult to assess accurately the likely impact of this external environment. Hence, managers usually focus on its key character-istics. These are often categorised as: 1) uncertainty; 2) dyna-mism; 3) complexity; and 4) munificence.

Uncertainty
Uncertainty refers to a lack of information. This makes it difficult to predict what or when something will happen. The higher the level of uncertainty, the more time managers need to spend monitoring their environment. This monitoring is necessary to help them:

▶ assess the implications of possible changes for the short, medium and long-term objectives of the company

▶ devise strategies for overcoming any problems that may arise.

Organisations need adequate and clear information about crucial variables in their environment. These include:

▶ the activities of their rivals

▶ possible increases in the costs of raw materials

▶ the relationship between organisational actions and environmental responses

▶ customer requirements and levels of customer satisfaction

▶ the time needed to collect and analyse information on these points.

Uncertainty can never be entirely eliminated, but it can be greatly reduced.

Dynamism
Dynamism reflects the rate and predictability of change in an organisation's environment. Stable organisations result from a slow and relatively predictable rate of change. Instability occurs when change is fast and relatively unpredictable. The greater the instability the more important frequent and effective monitoring becomes. Organisations must also be willing, and able, to react quickly to changing consumer desires and needs.

Complexity
Complexity refers to the number of environmental cues critical to an organisation's ability to function effectively. The high levels of activity involved need to be closely monitored. This affects the costs and quality of the inputs required. However, plans are usually constrained by supply difficulties. Homogeneous environments contain a relatively small number of similar items. Heterogeneous environments contain a large number of dissimilar items. This makes them more difficult to manage.

Munificence
Munificence refers to how well the environment can support sustained growth and stability. The amount of resources available and their accessibility to organisations are important issues. Unfortunately, if resources are plentiful they tend to attract other organisations. Access to resources depends on how well the values and goals of organisations match those of important resource suppliers. It will also depend on the types of transformation processes the organisation uses.

Forces within an organisation's environment
What type of forces are we discussing? It is difficult to be precise but, as a general rule, they may be classified as:

▶ other organisations that are concerned with the supply of human resources, finance and raw materials; consumers; and competitors

▶ regulatory bodies such as law courts, tribunals and watchdogs. These are concerned with monitoring and regulating the behaviour of organisations

▶ social trends and standards that govern an organisation's moral and ethical behaviour

▶ technology that changes the means by which an organisation produces its goods or services.

Strategies for managing environmental dependence

As we have seen, organisations cannot avoid being affected by their external environment. What they can do is develop ways of reducing the impact of that environment on their operations. Common ways an organisation can do this include the following:

1. Collecting information about its environment. It can then use this to anticipate possible actions. It can also use the data to help it forecast or predict future actions, often through the use of statistical models.

2. Reaching favourable agreements by means of lobbying, appointing people to relevant boards and projecting an acceptable image within its environment. It could also try to *improve* its image within the environment. This can be achieved by engaging appropriate staff or agencies. It could also join appropriate trade associations and engage in political activity, such as pressure groups.

3. Establishing sufficient control over people and supplies to reduce uncertainty and risk. This can be achieved by contracts, stockpiling resources, owning its own resources, rationing goods in high demand, diversifying into different markets or engaging in joint ventures with other organisations.

4. Taking action to reduce the impact of fluctuations, such as holding sales during slow periods or offering cheaper rates off peak.

The success of any strategy obviously depends on the situation the organisation is in. However, organisations can manoeuvre themselves into a favourable position if they are flexible and adaptable. As these are important issues, they need to be considered in great detail.

Environmental issues

Like technology, environmental issues are subject to rapid change. These issues can relate to:

▶ a specific organisation
▶ an industry
▶ a country.

In many instances the same issue can apply to all three. Pollution is an example of this (e.g. a particular organisation may be accused of the unsafe management of chemicals). However, environmental issues can also apply to whole industries, and some countries are less concerned with pollution than others. Other environmental issues relate to the type of raw materials used by organisations, employees' working conditions and the maintenance of land and buildings.

The question of environmental issues is closely related to such concerns as organisational objectives, ethics and control. These in turn are related to factors such as organisational structures, funding, the products and services provided, size, diversity and geographical territories. They are also related to issues discussed elsewhere in this chapter on technology and aspects of the external environment in general.

Environmental issues should not be considered in isolation. They arise from changes in technology, legal practices, social trends and other factors discussed throughout the book. The most fruitful way to tackle such issues is to focus on particular aspects of an organisation's operations that lend themselves to closer inspection. These should be considered in relation to:

▶ the impact an organisation has on its environment
▶ the impact the environment, or part of it, has on an organisation.

Tutorial

Progress questions
1. Why is technology now advancing at such a rapid rate?

2. Why is it important to consider how people and machines can work together?

3. Why do organisations need to pay attention to changes in their external environment?

Seminar discussion
1. Discuss ways in which people skills can be maintained in the face of increasing mechanisation and automation.

2. Discuss how organisations can more accurately predict factors relating to their own external environment.

Practical assignment
Select an organisation and investigate the problems it has experienced following the introduction of new technology. Suggest how these problems could have been avoided.

Study, revision and exam tips
1. As you read through this chapter, try to relate the key points to other aspects of organisations.

2. Try to keep up to date on technological and environmental issues to provide yourself with a practical viewpoint to the issues raised in this chapter.

4

Individuals

One-minute summary – The human element is the most difficult to control and predict yet the most crucial factor for an organisation's success. How individuals see their position in the organisation is of vital importance to the contributions they make. How they perceive themselves is partly based on the leadership skills of their managers, and partly on what the employees bring to the organisation. This in turn depends on such factors as their expectations, motivations, prior experience and values. The chapter will help you to understand:

- ▶ individuals' attitudes, values and expectations
- ▶ individuals' perceptions, motivation and learning needs
- ▶ how an organisation gets the best out of its employees
- ▶ leadership
- ▶ the individual and decision-making
- ▶ psychological contracts.

Individuals' attitudes, values and expectations

How people perceive their roles within an organisation has a very important bearing on how well or not they perform their tasks. To help us understand this, we need to focus on people's attitudes, values and expectations.

Attitudes
Everyone has an opinion or viewpoint on the events and situations that affect his or her life. An attitude refers to a relatively stable set of interests, opinions or purposes, and attitudes are often deep-rooted and difficult to change.

In the workplace, people will have attitudes about:

- ▶ the organisation itself
- ▶ the structures and hierarchy
- ▶ the rules and regulations
- ▶ different sets or groups of workers
- ▶ the organisation's culture.

Since they are difficult to change, organisations should take people's attitudes into account when recruiting and selecting employees. They could obtain information about an applicant's attitudes by asking him or her to:

- ▶ write about him or herself

- ▶ complete a range of psychological tests

- ▶ answer certain types of questions during an interview

- ▶ complete a series of tests and role plays at an assessment centre

- ▶ complete specific attitude scales.

None of these measures, however, will guarantee the selection of employees with particular kinds of attitudes. They will, on the other hand, indicate how closely applicants' views match those of the organisation.

Values
A value is often considered to be a quantitative measure or standard. If viewed in this way, a value should be relatively easy to understand and to calculate. An example would be the monetary value of a product or service or how much value a customer places on an item.

The qualitative aspect of value is far more difficult to define as it is concerned with individual judgements (for example, on the worth of an employee to a company, or how much an employee values his or her job or workmates).

In many instances value can be measured in both quantitative and qualitative terms. For example, the value of an employee to an organisation can be judged by:

- ▶ his or her salary
- ▶ bonuses
- ▶ perks
- ▶ status
- ▶ a performance review
- ▶ informal comments about his or her contributions to the team.

The value an employee places on his or her job or the companionship of colleagues is more difficult to measure. Often this can only be identified through informal discussion or through the employee's behaviour patterns.

If we take a wider perspective, employees bring sets of values into the workplace, and these may clash with organisational values. The most common clashes concern issues such as employee participation, promotion routes, equal opportunities and the environment.

Expectations

These refer to the anticipation of particular outcomes – rewards or penalties – related to something done or said. Future outcomes are often predicted from past experience.

In the workplace, some expectations are based on specific arrangements, such as rates of pay, holidays and work schedules. Other expectations are based on a person's experience of reactions made to certain types of comment or actions.

When employees join an organisation, they probably have certain expectations of what it is like to work there. They may also have expectations of how quickly they will be promoted, of being delegated to work in a team or of foreign travel. Workers will, therefore, become dissatisfied if their expectations are consistently not met.

Expectations are often based on desires rather than informed predictions, and this often results in disappointment. The more employees' expectations are in line with those of their organisation, the more likely they are to be met.

Individuals' perceptions, motivation and learning needs

Perception

Perception is the process of recognising or identifying something; of becoming aware of objects, qualities or relations. To perceive, we need to receive information from our senses (sight, hearing, smell, taste and touch) and to interpret these sensations. We can then use these interpretations to react to what we perceive.

Perception is not something that happens to us but is an active process. Therefore how we perceive things is influenced by a number of factors, including:

▶ our past experiences
▶ the clarity of our sensations
▶ our perception of others
▶ the amount of contradictory information we receive
▶ our ability to select from a mass of sensory information
▶ our needs and motivations.

At first, perception may not appear particularly relevant to workplace behaviour. If you think back, however, to earlier chapters and sections you should find many examples of the important role played by perception in the effective working of organisations. Some of these might include:

▶ how well individuals work together as a team
▶ an individual's reactions to occurrences in the workplace
▶ the reaction of team members to different leadership styles
▶ how well individuals accept new technology
▶ how individuals view themselves and others.

Motivation

Motivation is the general term used to describe those things that drive us forward and that give us the incentive to act in a certain way. In other words, why do we set and strive for certain goals? What pushes us and gives direction to our behaviour?

Understanding what motivates members of their team is a

complex and difficult challenge for managers. However, although motivation differs between individuals, there are some things that are common motivators to us all. These include the desires for:

- ▶ security
- ▶ financial rewards
- ▶ recognition
- ▶ power
- ▶ self-development
- ▶ appreciation
- ▶ achievement.

Individuals, however, tend to give different priorities to different needs and, although these are relatively stable, priorities can change with time and circumstances.

Knowing what motivates people should help organisations to meet their needs and, ideally, the needs of individuals will match those of the organisation for which they work. If there is a mismatch, problems are likely to occur: a contented workforce is likely to be more productive than a disgruntled one.

Learning
We learn by experience – by responding to particular situations and the consequences of these. Learning takes place when we can reproduce a particular response – when a change in our behaviour becomes relatively permanent. Learning is also an ongoing process.

When employees first join an organisation they should receive a comprehensive induction. This will include:

- ▶ information about important organisational policies such as health and safety, equal opportunities, bullying and harassment and environmental issues

- ▶ company rules, regulations and procedures

- ▶ their statutory rights and obligations as employees

- ▶ the layout of the building

► an organisation chart

► task requirements.

Following the induction, relevant training and development should be made available to all employees. At the lower levels of the organisation this might relate mainly to product knowledge and procedural changes. At managerial level it should also include the updating of professional and technical knowledge, increasing managerial skills and obtaining a wider understanding of business issues in general.

Some companies operate a mentor system for new recruits and promoted staff. This is usually a temporary situation where senior or more experienced staff help and advise others. Organisations that fail to acknowledge the importance of continuous learning are likely to fall behind their competitors.

How an organisation gets the best out of its employees

To some extent, the content of this section is dealt with elsewhere in the book. However, it is useful to draw this information together here and to consolidate it under its own specific heading.

As we have seen, employees do not cease to be individuals when they enter the workplace. They bring with them deep-rooted attitudes, values, ways of perceiving, desires and needs. They also have their own targets and frequently encounter obstacles on the road to achieving these.

While people can be viewed as assets or liabilities, they are often expensive to employ. And managing people is usually far more difficult than managing physical or financial resources. This is one reason why some organisations have introduced varying degrees of mechanisation and automation. As we saw in Chapter 3, machines do not require job satisfaction, pay rises, holidays or lunch breaks.

If people are such a problem, why are they still considered so valuable? There are a number of reasons for this:

▶ technology is still not sufficiently advanced to replace people entirely

▶ people provide ideas and inspiration which are crucial to company success

▶ people prefer to mix with other people than simply to interact with machines

▶ people play a dual role – as employees and as consumers. Without paid employment sales would fall.

Organisations use a variety of methods to get the best out of their employees. The methods used depend very much on the employees' needs and what companies are prepared to do to satisfy these. Common methods that have been tried, however, with varying degrees of success, include:

▶ various financial incentive schemes, such as bonus payments, profit-sharing and staff discounts

▶ perks, such as a company car, private health insurance, pension schemes, mobile telephones and subsidised staff restaurants

▶ worker participation in decision-making through works committees, shareholder voting rights, representatives on boards of directors, suggestion schemes and involvement in working parties

▶ the provision of a pleasant and secure working environment

▶ opportunities for social interaction

▶ opportunities for promotion and fair promotion policies

▶ the provision of an organisational culture that values employees and that makes them aware of this.

However, no one policy or practice will harmonise working relationships between departments and grades of staff, and so a combination of methods is usually required. The methods used should be continuously monitored and evaluated, and appropriate changes made as required.

Leadership

Leaders are responsible for the direction and control of the people and resources under their jurisdiction. In business organisations they are referred to as supervisors, managers or directors. The exact title will depend on their level of authority and the organisational structure.

It is useful to begin a discussion of leadership by trying to identify the main skills a good or effective leader should have. There are too many of these to provide a comprehensive review here, but some of the key attributes are listed below:

▶ a good listener
▶ approachable
▶ able to delegate
▶ flexible and adaptable
▶ a good communicator
▶ able and willing to make decisions
▶ fair and non-judgemental
▶ a good motivator
▶ able to command the respect of staff
▶ an able negotiator.

This list could be much longer but already the complexity of the leadership role should have become clear.

Few leaders will possess all the necessary leadership skills, and many will have important deficiencies. Some will be completely unsuited to the tasks demanded of them. Others will possess many of the attributes related to effective leadership prior to their appointment. Yet others will need to have these developed. It is, however, difficult to identify particular personality traits that make an effective leader. Of more use here is to consider the style of leadership people adopt.

Task versus relationship leaders

Like most aspects of personality, it is best to consider these two aspects of leadership style – task and relationship – along sliding scales rather than as absolute categories. Task-orientated leaders place goal achievement as their main priority. However, while all leaders have to meet objectives, it is not wise to do so at the expense of harmonious working relations. If this style of leadership is too extreme, employee turnover and grievance levels are likely to increase. Relationship-orientated leaders, on the other hand, are more concerned with establishing and maintaining rapport and trust within their teams.

Leaders who are at the extreme end of the task or relationship dimension are most likely to experience difficulties with their teams. Effective organisations need a balance of both types of leader. One solution is to have pairs of leaders (such as managers and deputy managers) with different preferred leadership styles.

Styles of management
Managers adopt various styles, which reflect their approaches to leadership:

1. *Authoritarian managers* see their role as one of issuing orders that must be obeyed by their staff. In an extreme form this is unlikely to work. Worker morale and production levels tend to fall, while staff turnover increases.

2. *Bureaucratic managers* tend to be slow and overly cautious in making decisions. They rely on procedures and rules, committees and working parties.

3. *Democratic managers* try to involve their staff in the decision-making process. This should result in more commitment and a greater range of ideas being put forward.

4. *Laissez-faire managers* appear to abdicate any responsibility for control and decision-making. They may have been promoted for their professional or technical skills. Often they lack leadership skills or the interest to manage effectively.

5. *Paternal managers* try to create a family atmosphere while they retain overall control. This management style is usually associated with small organisations.

Formal versus informal leadership
Formal leaders are those appointed to specific positions within an

organisation, and their authority and power are related to the roles they have been appointed to fulfil. Formal leaders can be identified by reference to a company's organisation chart. This will also show their position within the hierarchy. Formal leaders should adhere to the company's rules and regulations with respect to the resources and people in their domain. Employees who refuse to accept the authority of a formal leader can be disciplined.

Informal leaders owe their position to their influence over their fellow workers. This may result from their popularity or from them possessing particular knowledge or skills. Informal leaders may emerge in situations when their own particular experience and expertise are required. Alternatively, they could exert consistent and general influence over their colleagues.

Some formal leaders may feel threatened by informal leaders. However, shrewd managers will make sure both types of leader work together as a partnership.

The individual and decision-making

The role played by individuals in the decision-making process will depend on a number of factors:

▶ the nature of the organisation – its structure, traditions, culture and goals

▶ the grade of employee

▶ the desire of individuals to participate in decision-making

▶ the expertise and experience of individual employees

▶ the nature of the decision being made

▶ the decision-making processes and procedures.

All organisations have a chain of command that may be identified from their organisation charts. As we saw in Chapter 2, involvement in decision-making is usually hierarchical: major decisions are made and implemented at the top. Departmental managers and supervisors are then responsible for decisions in their own sections of the organisation.

We have already emphasised the importance of at least some degree of employee involvement in decision-making, and this is now acknowledged by many organisations. It is important to bear in mind, however, that decisions made at lower levels can have a cumulative impact on the overall effectiveness of the organisation.

The extent of employee involvement in decision-making depends on the organisation's culture. In top-down organisations, decisions flow downward from senior managers to the rest of the organisation. In extreme forms, there will be little or no opportunities for input from lower-grade managers or other employees. In bottom-up organisations, there are opportunities for staff at all levels to influence decision-making.

Psychological contracts

The word *contract* usually conjures up visions of precisely worded, formally structured legal documents. Today, few people would consider accepting a job unless it was accompanied by a contract of employment. This sets out the terms and conditions of employment and acts as a safeguard for both employers and employees.

Although legal protection is essential for employees, most of what happens in the workplace is difficult to define. A *psychological* contract is unwritten and, often, unconscious. It involves the expectation employers and employees have of each other.

The role of the organisation

Since organisations are the legal employer, ultimately individuals enter into psychological contracts with them. As we have already seen, individuals bring a complicated set of attitudes, beliefs and values into the workplace, and these form the basis for determining an individual's:

▶ level of commitment to the organisation

▶ expectations of what he or she will receive from the organisation.

Employee expectations usually relate to:

▶ their physical working conditions

▶ the requirements of the job

▶ the physical and mental demands of the job

▶ the nature of the choices open to them in carrying out their duties

▶ the ways in which authority will be exerted over them.

The most fruitful psychological contracts, therefore, will be those forged between organisations and individuals with similar goals and expectations. The more these differ, the more fraught will be the contract. Balanced contracts are essential if the employer/ employee relationship is to be harmonious.

The role of the manager

Although individuals are employed by an organisation, the psychological contract is usually forged with representatives of that organisation. In small organisations, this may be the owner or senior manager. In large organisations, employees are often managed by a number of people at different levels of the organisation.

The nature of a psychological contract implies it is between individuals rather than an intangible mass such as an organisation. If employees report to more than one manager, they are likely to have a psychological contract with each. These are likely to differ according to:

▶ the amount of authority a manager has

▶ a manager's leadership style

▶ how closely the needs and expectations of the employee meet those of the manager.

Contributions and inducements

If there are two parties to a contract, then each has to a role to play. If you are buying a house the person selling the house has the property and the buyer the financial means to purchase the house. As the buyer will have alternative options, the seller may offer inducements, such as a discount for a quick sale or the inclusion of carpets and curtains.

In a psychological contract, the employee contributes:

▶ his or her mental and physical effort
▶ acquired skills
▶ relevant experience
▶ loyalty to the organisation
▶ commitment to the organisation's goals.

On its part, an organisation can reward its employees with:

▶ an agreed salary

▶ bonus payments

▶ job security

▶ staff discount and other benefits

▶ status and promotion opportunities

▶ various job perks (such as a company car, free health insurance, pension schemes)

▶ appropriate training and development.

Which contributions and inducements apply will vary with individuals, job posts and organisations. If the balance between contributions and inducements is badly matched, this is likely to affect:

▶ the progression of an employee within an organisation

▶ the level of trust between the two parties

▶ the level of an employee's job satisfaction

▶ an employee's commitment in terms of attendance and time-keeping

▶ an employee's level of productivity

▶ the employment period (which can be curtailed on either side).

The balance of the psychological contract depends mainly on two factors:

1. the extent to which both parties (employee and organisation) feel their expectations have been met

2. agreement on what is actually to be exchanged.

Tutorial

Progress questions
1. Explain how a knowledge and understanding of individuals can assist employers to get the best out of their workforce.
2. Suggest ways in which employees, at all levels, can contribute to the decision-making process within their organisation.
3. How do psychological contracts differ from contracts of employment?

Seminar discussion
Each member of the seminar group should select an organisation and present information on key points that have emerged from this chapter. The points to be discussed will be decided by the seminar leader. The points presented can then be used to illustrate similarities and differences between organisations.

Practical assignment
Conduct surveys on one or more of the following issues:

▶ the degree of employee participation in decision-making
▶ the nature of psychological contracts
▶ leadership styles.

The survey could be used either as an in-depth investigation of a particular organisation or as a comparison between two or more organisations.

Study, revision and exam tips

1. Think of examples as you read through the various sections of this chapter.

2. Wherever possible, try to link the concepts and principles discussed in this chapter to organisations you know.

5

Groups

One-minute summary – Individuals within organisations do not operate in isolation. They are arranged into teams, sections, departments, branches and divisions. They rely on each other to perform their tasks and they influence each other's behaviour. In ideal situations, groups work in harmony. In reality, however, conflicts frequently occur as people vie for influence and power. To be successful, organisations need successful teams. In recognition of this, this chapter will help you to understand:

▶ the nature, formation and purpose of groups
▶ group dynamics
▶ how to build effective teams
▶ power, influence and decision-making
▶ conflict within and between groups.

The nature, formation and purpose of groups

The nature of groups
Throughout our lives we belong to a number of groups. These usually begin with the family and spread to school, friendship, sporting and social groups. In the workplace, groups are equally important although these are usually more formal and structured. In an organisational context, a group will have the following characteristics:

▶ it must comprise two or more people
▶ the people comprising the group must be inter-related in some way
▶ this inter-relationship must be organised and systematic
▶ the relationships should be functional

67

► there should be accepted standards of behaviour within the group
► the group must have a common goal(s).

Groups may be classified as either formal or informal. Formal groups are those created by an organisation for a specific purpose. This may be to work on a production line, in a temporary project team or in a section or department. Informal groups are created by individuals with common interests and needs. These generally have less rigid structures and their purposes may similarly be less clear.

Group formation
Like any other type of relationship, groups must go through various stages of development. Sometimes these stages have different labels attached to them but, however they are described, in essence they are basically the same.

The initial or formation stage
This stage begins when group members first come together. During this stage the members need to become acquainted with each other to discover their strengths and weaknesses. They need to establish ground rules that are acceptable to everyone, and they need to explore their task and allocate roles. They must also elect a leader, if one has not been officially appointed. Unofficial leaders also start to emerge at this stage.

The 'getting to know you' stage
This stage often involves conflict and disagreement between members. Relationships are formed, and members either stick to or revise their opinions of their colleagues. To survive this stage and move forward, compromises need to be made and tentative action plans agreed.

The establishing relationships and rules stage
This stage involves focusing on developing group norms – deciding on acceptable rules and behaviours. Individuals need to start thinking like a team and to identify with the group. Roles within the group become clearer, and members focus on their targets.

Unofficial leaders will be reviewed and changed if necessary.

The performance stage
Meeting group objectives now assumes priority. Any conflict that emerges at this stage should be easy to deal with. This should be the most effective and most productive stage in the team's development. If problems occur groups should now be mature enough to deal with them.

What happens next depends on group membership and circumstances. If there is a change of membership, the group may need to return to the earlier stage of formation. Alternatively, if the group task is achieved and further tasks are not allocated, the group may be disbanded.

The purpose of groups
From your own experience you should be aware that groups are formed, and stay together, for a specific reason. Some groups are created as temporary solutions to a particular problem. Others are part of an organisation's permanent structure. The group's purpose is dictated by the group's membership and its tasks. The purpose of groups in general, however, is much less easy to establish.

There has always been some form of 'work group'. In more primitive times, these groups would have comprised family members or members of the same tribe or village. Even within these groups, tasks would have been allocated according to the ability, age, gender, experience and skills of the members.

As societies became more complex and people started working outside the home, the need for groups became more pressing. While the basic foundations for effective group working still applied, they now needed to become more formalised. With the development of large, complex organisations, labour finally became formalised into divisions and specialisations.

In a company these divisions can be identified by reference to the company's organisation chart. Some groups may be large, representing a division, branch, department or section. Each of these major categories, however, is likely to be broken down further into much smaller groups or work teams.

The main purpose of such divisions and subdivisions is to provide working units of an effective size. More specifically, the general purpose of groups is to:

▶ provide a pool of ideas, perspectives and suggestions
▶ share information between members
▶ bring together a variety of abilities, experience and skills
▶ provide opportunities for specialisation
▶ reduce the duplication of tasks and resources
▶ enable group members to stimulate, help and support each other
▶ involve more people in the decision-making process
▶ reduce the burden on senior managers.

Group dynamics

In organisations, as in other areas of our lives, most social interaction takes place in groups, and individuals often act very differently in the different groups they belong to. Also, when the membership of a group changes, so can the group's dynamics. Group dynamics, although usually readily identifiable, are, however, difficult to describe. Ways of describing them include:

▶ how people interact within a group
▶ the chemistry that exists between groups of people
▶ how people work together in groups
▶ the harnessing of energy within a group.

The dynamics of a group will depend on factors such as:

▶ membership of a group at a particular time
▶ the tasks group members have to perform
▶ how groups are structured to accomplish their tasks
▶ the motivation of group members towards their tasks
▶ the relationship of group members to each other
▶ the rules adopted by a group to enable them to complete

their tasks
- ▶ the leadership and other roles allocated to group members
- ▶ the rewards that are a consequence of being a member of a particular group.

However we define or explain group dynamics we have to appreciate the fact that, if the dynamics are right, groups usually work effectively. If the dynamics are wrong, however, disharmony and conflict may result. When this occurs, groups become dysfunctional. It is, therefore, in an organisation's interests to encourage and nurture positive group dynamics.

How to build effective teams

Building effective teams relates closely to group dynamics: in other words, how can we make groups work together effectively? 'Team building' is the term used to describe a common method employed to improve group dynamics. This involves a process of diagnosis, intervention, monitoring and evaluation:

1. The *diagnosis* stage considers the current situation. It aims to discover what is preventing a team from achieving its full potential.

2. The *intervention* stage involves strategies aimed at rectifying any deficiencies or problems diagnosed.

3. The *monitoring* stage makes sure any changes made are checked regularly, and that feedback is provided to team members.

4. The *evaluation* stage involves weighing up the positive and negative results of any changes made. The ultimate aim is to measure the effectiveness of change within the team.

As we saw earlier, the members chosen for a group and how they interact together are crucial for the team's success. It is commonly believed that effective groups need to contain a balance of personality types. However, obtaining the right blend of group members is a very difficult task. This is true even if teams are built with a specific purpose in mind. And many teams that are already in existence will not have a good balance of personality types, expertise and experience.

There is no one simple way to build a balanced, happy, effective and productive team. However, techniques to develop effective teams include:

▶ focusing on a particular aspect(s) of team building, such as trust, behaviour awareness and interpersonal skills

▶ studying how teams interact with each other and working to improve this

▶ helping team members to become more sensitive towards the needs of others

▶ developing negotiating skills among team members to help them achieve their personal goals

▶ identifying the preferred roles team members would like to play, where the gaps are and how these can be filled

▶ comparing the personalities of team members to those of certain animals (a lion, a fox, etc.). This helps to depersonalise an individual's particular characteristics.

Power, influence and decision-making

In many respects, influence and power refer to the same thing. They both involve affecting the attitude, or behaviour, of others. However, having power is usually considered to mean someone being in a position of authority. Having influence, on the other hand, is seen more as being in a position to sway or affect the decisions of those in control.

Influence and power
In simple terms, power involves the ability to influence the behaviour of others and to exert control over the environment. This can extend to making people do things they would prefer not to do. The desire for power may also be related to a desire to help

an organisation to meet its goals. However it is defined, power usually means being in control of resources. Taking organisations as an example, those with power are usually those who have financial control.

Influence is often viewed as someone being in a position to have a bearing on outcomes through his or her relationship with those in power. Influence may be the result of having valuable expertise or of being able to make effective use of interpersonal skills.

We have seen that people with power can exert pressure to make others do things, perhaps against their will. Power can bring about two types of change:

1. *direct* change, by altering an individual's behaviour
2. *indirect* change, through a third party or a group.

Sources of power within an organisation may be based on:

▶ the ability to reward people
▶ the capacity to inflict harm or punishment
▶ the role an individual plays within an organisation
▶ the individual's status or position within an organisation
▶ the possession of particular expertise or experience
▶ personal characteristics that make others want to please an individual.

Different sources of power will be appropriate to different situations. For example, power based on role or status is most relevant to people working in hierarchical organisations. Power based on expertise and experience is also relevant within a hierarchical organisation but also in situations where a professional is consulted for his or her expertise. Power based on personal characteristics, on the other hand, is not necessarily linked to role or status and usually applies to informal leaders.

Being aware of the main sources of power can provide individuals with knowledge about how to acquire that power. Examples of this include working hard to gain promotion or exploiting your expertise and experience.

The unequal distribution of power is inevitable, both within organisations and in society at large. Therefore power should be used sensibly and constructively. However, it can also be abused. If this happens, an organisation is unlikely to operate effectively in the longer term.

Decision-making

Decision-making is the process of choosing between alternatives. This may refer to informed decisions made by people in authority. Alternatively, it may involve participation by people at varying levels within an organisation. The type of decisions involved can also vary. Some may be major, strategic decisions that will affect the organisation and its external environment. Others may be relatively minor decisions that affect mainly members of a particular section or team.

In organisations, all managers make decisions. The type of decisions they make is related to their post and the responsibilities linked to this. Senior managers are concerned with long-term strategic decisions. These usually involve major capital investment and carry varying degrees of risk. Middle managers generally make more tactical decisions and implement strategic decisions. Operational decisions on the day-to-day running of an organisation can be made at lower management and supervisory levels.

Whatever the level or nature of a decision, it is wise to go through a series of steps or stages. If any of these stages is missed out, the decisions made are likely to be flawed:

Stage 1 – identify the problem.
Stage 2 – consider a range of options to solve the problem.
Stage 3 – evaluate the options and select the most appropriate.
Stage 4 – implement and monitor the option selected.

Although managers within organisations face different types of decisions, these may be clustered as follows:

▶ *Crisis decisions* that need immediate attention and action. Common examples include a financial crisis, a dramatic decrease in sales or a health scare relating to a particular product.

▶ *Issue decisions* that are less urgent. These could relate to a need to widen the geographical customer base, to standardise machinery or procedures between plants or to implement new legislation.

▶ *Strategic decisions* to take advantage of opportunities for expansion or to launch a new product or service.

Conflict within and between groups

As we have seen in previous sections, relationships within and between groups are not always harmonious. This is not necessarily a cause for concern. Some level of disharmony is probably useful to prevent groups becoming stale and unproductive. However, too much disagreement can permanently damage relationships and become a barrier to progress.

The nature of conflict

We all have had experience of conflict. Conflict results when individuals or groups oppose the actions or wishes of others. If conflict is allowed to develop it can produce tensions between the opposing parties. Often the problem lies much deeper than the supposed reason for opposition. It usually involves fundamental differences in perceptions, beliefs and goals.

Within organisations, the main causes of conflict may include:

▶ different beliefs and viewpoints
▶ disagreements about decisions that need to be made
▶ disagreement over how to allocate scarce resources
▶ differences over goals or targets
▶ differences over priorities
▶ perceived inequalities of workload
▶ communication breakdowns
▶ differences in personality and values
▶ differences in experience and expertise
▶ unfairly or badly designed reward systems.

Many of these sources of conflict have their roots in individual differences and, because of this, conflict between individuals is almost inevitable. The practice of organisations clustering people into work teams will also increase the potential for conflict. It also provides a base from which conflict can be nurtured.

Conflict within groups

Groups in the workplace are formed artificially to assist production. People are usually allocated to groups according to their job roles, their specialisms or their geographical proximity. If we refer back to the section on the formation of groups, it may seem that conflict is more likely during the early stages. However, changing membership and situations mean the threat of conflict is always present.

In the workplace, all groups have a set purpose. The need to achieve group objectives, therefore, places individuals under great pressure to conform to group norms. Resistance to such pressure can lead to a lack of cohesion or, ultimately, to poor performance. Bearing this in mind, it is important to identify the main sources of conflict within groups:

▶ members of the group may have conflicting goals or goal priorities
▶ personality differences between group members
▶ disagreement with the group leader
▶ the development of subgroups
▶ a lack of commitment to the group and its goals
▶ loyalty to a previous group or a desire to join another group
▶ resentment by group members about their role in the group
▶ a lack of stability due to frequent changes of goals or membership.

To resolve conflict within groups, it is essential to make sure all members accept group norms. To achieve this it may be necessary to:

▶ change the group goals
▶ change the group leader
▶ transfer uncooperative members to other groups

▶ bring in new members who are more likely to co-operate
▶ change the situation that has led to conflict
▶ encourage members to support higher-level goals
▶ try to work out an acceptable compromise
▶ try temporarily to suppress the conflict until a solution can be found
▶ focus attention on conflict with another group
▶ devise solutions that allow all parties to reach their goals
▶ investigate the conflict and make a rational decision.

Conflict between groups

In many respects this is similar to conflict within groups. The interdependent structure of most organisations means groups work closely with each other. The sources of conflict in one group can often spread to create similar conflict in others. However, there are important differences between *inter* (between) and *intra* (within) group conflicts:

▶ groups may be competing against each other for scarce resources
▶ group productivity may affect bonus payments and other rewards
▶ group performance may affect the promotion chances of members
▶ groups may become the focal point of members' loyalty
▶ group performance may determine status within the organisation.

The nature of intergroup conflict may help to improve relationships within groups. This occurs when group members rally to defeat outside opposition. It usually results in greater cohesion, co-operation and productivity within a particular group.

Conflict and the organisation

As pointed out elsewhere in this chapter, organisations can create the conflict they seek to reduce or resolve. How can this happen? You have probably discovered by now that it is impossible to treat problems in a vacuum. If problems occur within an organisation, it is likely the organisation is to blame. This can happen in a number of ways:

- ▶ organisational structures can create problems within and between groups

- ▶ poor communication within the organisation can cause uncertainty, dissatisfaction and conflict

- ▶ limited opportunities for workers to become involved in decision-making can create misunderstandings, resentment and conflict

- ▶ the organisational culture may not encourage effective teams to develop and thrive

- ▶ the management styles favoured by an organisation may create problems

- ▶ recruitment, selection, job design and job allocation practices may create conflict

- ▶ the strategies used to help develop effective teams may be inadequate.

While it is useful and perhaps necessary to discuss groups as a separate entity, we need to bear in mind that groups are a very small part of the whole. To study groups effectively we need to place them back inside that whole. We need to view them as part of the organisation to which they belong.

Tutorial

Progress questions

1. Go back to earlier chapters. Try to identify the type of groups that would be appropriate for particular parts of an organisation.

2. Explain, with examples, how intragroup conflict differs from intergroup conflict.

3. How can widening the consultation process within an organisation reduce group conflict?

Seminar discussion
1. Investigate and discuss how team-building techniques could be used to make your seminar group work more effectively.

2. Each member of the seminar group could investigate problems of conflict within a task group with which he or she is familiar. This should, preferably, be in an organisation where he or she has worked.

Practical assignment
Conduct a survey in a workplace of your choice to find out:

▶ what people like most/least about working in teams
▶ what the main sources of conflict are within teams
▶ how conflicts within teams may be resolved.

Study, revision and exam tips
1. Get into the habit of linking topics together and trying to see how they fit into the whole subject area (for example, how organisational structures can create conflict).

2. Make an effort to relate theory to practice whenever possible (for example, become more aware of organisational problems when you are in work).

6

Culture and the External Environment

One-minute summary – Individuals are recognisable by their physical attributes and their personality characteristics. In a similar way, organisations can be recognised by their structures and culture. Together, these help to determine how an organisation interacts with its external environment and the impact this environment has on the company concerned. This chapter will help you to understand:

▶ the nature and types of organisational culture
▶ the importance of culture
▶ culture and structure
▶ the effective transmission of culture
▶ culture and the external environment.

The nature and types of organisational culture

What is organisational culture?

Culture is traditionally associated with societies and groups of people in society. It refers to the pattern of development reflected in people's beliefs, ideology, knowledge, laws, norms, rituals and values. If we transfer this concept to organisations, it allows us to apply this notion of belief systems to business practice.

All organisations have a culture, and how an organisation's image is perceived by the public at large is crucial for the organisation's success. In some organisations, the culture is strong, cohesive and easily recognisable. In others it is fragmented and difficult to identify.

Corporate culture (see below) usually develops as an *ethos* (a system of collective beliefs). This is created and sustained by social processes such as images, rituals and symbols. It is important for employees to be genuinely committed to their corporate culture. This helps them to work together effectively as a team. However, such harmony is difficult to achieve. In some cases, employees may appear to conform when in fact they have no genuine belief in the system. This is a serious threat to the organisation: conflict is best kept in the open where it can be resolved.

Types of organisational culture

The dominant culture in an organisation is generally linked to other factors, such as the organisation's purpose, structure, tradition and position in the marketplace. In view of this, there are many different ways in which an organisation's culture can be classified. A few examples are provided below.

Traditional

A traditional culture is one where there are long-standing shared beliefs, norms and values. Organisations with this type of culture are either content with their current approach or afraid to change.

Entrepreneurial

Entrepreneurial cultures are associated with a strong desire for growth and change. This type of organisation tends to be confident about its current position and its ability to further its position within the marketplace.

Bureaucratic

A bureaucratic culture works to retain the status quo. This type of organisation tends to react to situations rather than be innovative and proactive.

Complacent

A complacent culture is often associated with organisations that are currently in a strong position and that do not see the need for change.

Social

Social culture refers to organisations operating (usually) in the public or voluntary sectors. Profit is either not a goal or not of prime importance.

Whatever type of culture an organisation adopts, it is important for it to recognise the extent to which that culture:

► helps it to achieve its organisational goals
► is genuinely accepted among its employees
► is viewed positively by customers and clients
► allows it to be flexible and responsive to change.

Culture and social reality

Culture may be viewed as a way of constructing reality: culture helps people to see and make sense of particular events, objects, actions, words or situations in distinctive ways. Once developed, these patterns of understanding can also help them to interpret their own behaviour.

This is difficult to recognise when everything is running smoothly: it only becomes clear when there is a disruption to what we view as normal behaviour. When this happens, the consequences of not acting normally become apparent. All systems, whether an organisation or systems in society at large, need to be *accepted*. Without this they cannot survive.

To understand a culture we should study its social norms and customs. In many instances, we are too involved in our own particular cultures to view them objectively. This is one reason why visiting another country or organisation helps us to see our own culture more clearly. People who change jobs or work abroad for a time need to learn about these new cultures if they are to succeed. This does not mean that cultures can be learnt by following simple rules and regulations. Understanding and interpretation are still crucial.

It is useful to view culture as dynamic and active rather than static and rigid. Culture can, and does, change along with changes in the wider environment. Therefore, the process of constructing a social reality is ongoing. It is continually created, and recreated, by the people who live and work in the social systems involved.

The importance of culture

An organisation's culture is an important means of achieving harmony among employees: of making sure everyone is striving for the same goals. It is also a useful way of communicating an organisation's beliefs and values to those outside.

Influencing organisational culture

An organisation's culture is usually determined and transmitted from the top down to its various structural levels. To see how this works, it is useful to refer back to the organisation charts discussed in Chapter 2. In a top-down system, the norms, beliefs and values of the senior managers are a vital ingredient to the organisation's culture.

It is difficult to isolate an organisation's culture from the culture of the wider society in which it operates. For example, the different cultures of countries such as the USA, Britain, France and Japan will strongly influence the culture of organisations within their boundaries. Conversely, if a Japanese company opens a plant in Britain it will bring some of its national culture to that plant.

Organisational culture is not just affected by current events. It is also influenced by what was happening – internally and externally – at the time of the organisation's formation. Contemporary UK society is dominated by large organisations.

Our working lives are largely governed by:

▶ timetables
▶ rules and regulations
▶ authority figures
▶ policies.

The rituals, beliefs, norms and values associated with these differ between organisations and between societies. However, it is likely that workers from earlier eras would recognise similarities between them.

People working in similar jobs, organisations and industries are likely to share many experiences and expectations. Belonging to particular teams, sections and divisions also requires adherence to the culture of those particular subdivisions. These may conform to, or clash with, the overall culture of the organisation.

Managerial style is a major determinant of how an organisation's culture evolves and is conveyed to employees. Senior managers are uniquely placed to help develop value systems, codes of ethics and behaviour. Informal leaders also play an important role in the creation and dissemination of an organisation's culture. They do this mainly through example and influence rather than by authority or power.

In some instances employees may welcome, and even embrace, their organisation's culture. In others, they need to be persuaded by incentives or penalties. Motives such as loyalty, fear or the desire for reward will affect both the workers' behaviour and their true feelings about the organisation. Generally, culture is not imposed but develops gradually through social interaction.

Maintaining corporate culture

Organisations employ many experts to help them to cultivate and maintain their corporate culture. Many modern organisations also use rational arguments to help them legitimise their public image. A major strength of corporate culture is that it allows the symbolic and the rational to exist alongside each other. Corporate culture binds the organisation together. By emphasising shared beliefs it provides a means of focusing energy towards the achievement of goals. Although managers play a key role in doing this, all employees have important roles to play.

The dominant leadership within an organisation also influences the culture the organisation adopts. An authoritarian company will expect obedience from its employees. A more democratic company will encourage employee involvement, consultation and commitment.

Organisations also select their structure to help them govern in the style they have chosen. This in turn helps them to disseminate their culture both inside the organisation and in their external environment. Firms try to organise their environments in the same way as they organise their internal operations.

Cultural is also an important factor in helping organisation to embrace change. Organisations do not simply change their technologies, structures and functions but also the whole process of their culture. If we can recognise this, it will help us to view organisations as dynamic, living entities.

Culture and structure

Rituals are embedded in the formal structure of an organisation. They play a crucial role in helping to convey the values that shape an organisation's goals.

Contemporary organisations are essential for our survival. Everything is now sectionalised and specialised: jobs, sections, departments, organisations and even industries. This trend has increased with advances in technology. As a result, all sectors of society and organisations are inter-related and dependent upon each other. Jobs and behaviours become so habitual we only question what we do and how we do it when something unusual happens.

Although the focus of this book is organisations, their culture is closely linked with the societies they inhabit. Goals, objectives, purpose and structures may differ but industries and societies strongly affect organisational culture. Cultural differences are also linked to particular occupational groups.

Corporate culture

As we have seen, corporate culture is based on shared beliefs, meanings, norms, rituals and values. The term 'corporate culture' is misleading, however. Most organisations house many different and competing value systems rather than a uniform corporate culture. However, some degree of cohesion is essential if an organisation is to achieve its goals.

Many aspects of an organisation's culture are embedded in its rules, regulations, policies and structure. These help to determine how an organisation sees itself. They also help outsiders to make sense of a corporate culture. These indicators include:

▶ analysing day-to-day function and performance
▶ looking at how people interact with each other
▶ discovering what images are projected
▶ interpreting language and symbols.

Most organisational behaviour and structure have a strong historical base. This may not, however, be immediately apparent.

We need to look beyond the superficial to discover the reality. We also need to distinguish between the public image and what happens in private.

Organisational culture is not static. It can change with changes in leadership or circumstances. Mergers usually cause dramatic changes in culture as the dominant partner imposes their culture on the less powerful one. Staff will bear the brunt of such changes but customers and suppliers will also be affected. Internal challenges may occur. To manage change successfully, managers need to know their existing corporate culture: to understand how culture fits in with other aspects of the organisational jigsaw.

Corporate subcultures

We have already questioned the concept of a corporate culture. Divisions within an organisation may be based on professional groupings, social and ethnic backgrounds or product and functional splits. Each may have its own degree of cohesion. This is essential if an organisation is to achieve its goals, norms, language and ways of formalising business priorities. Some divisions may be informal or transitory. Others may be more institutionalised, such as the management versus worker divide. Some may be purely functional; others may reflect a battle for control.

A more realistic approach, therefore, is to view corporations as mini-societies containing various subcultures. These may take different forms and adopt different strategies. Examples include:

▶ a family traditional culture that stresses the need for everyone to work together towards a common goal

▶ a competitive culture that works towards dominance and excellence over other cultures

▶ a fragmented culture with different sections and groups having different aspirations and expectations.

Although subcultures are only to be expected and may in fact benefit an organisation, they should not be too divisive.

The effective transmission of culture

As we have seen, corporations may be viewed as mini-societies, each with an identifiable culture and subculture. The roots of these can usually be traced back to the corporation's origins. Hence, the characteristics of corporate culture vary. Examples include:

▶ a *paternalistic* culture that can be translated into a strict but caring leadership

▶ a *community spirit* culture that can be translated into a strong emphasis on teamwork

▶ a *work ethic* culture that can be translated into a drive towards high productivity, with an emphasis on loyalty to the organisation.

International companies can further complicate the situation. These usually bring with them traces of their national cultures. These may clash with the culture of the host country. For example, the British class culture is based on conflict between workers and management. Japanese organisations place more emphasis on co-operation and teamwork. In America, winning is of prime importance and competition is encouraged. Sound knowledge and understanding of foreign cultures are crucial for organisations operating outside their national boundaries.

Shared reality in organisations

Despite the existence of subcultures, organisations must make sure their employees share their main goals, visions and values if they are to succeed. This shared view of reality is transmitted through an organisation's processes, procedures and structures. To under-stand an organisation's culture we need to discover exactly how this reality is created, communicated and sustained. We also need to appreciate the changing nature of organisations and how this affects their culture.

Culture is a complex, evolving form of social practice. It is characterised by:

▶ internal and external influences

▶ changing patterns that are difficult to identify

▶ a reality that appears fragmented and superficial to outsiders

▶ a reality that appears hollow and mechanistic to those inside.

Corporate culture comprises a variety of features and practices that together reveal the views of the organisation's employees. Despite its importance, corporate culture is just one way of looking at organisations. Viewed in isolation, it is not an effective analytical tool.

Culture and the external environment

Organisations are an integral part of the external environment they inhabit. What happens outside their boundaries is a continual source of influence and concern. Organisations receive physical resources, staff and information from their external environment. These are used to provide particular goods and services that are then sold back to the external environment.

Organisations encounter problems when dealing with their environment. The nature and extent of these problems depend on such factors as:

▶ their position within the environment

▶ the image they are trying to project

▶ how acceptable they are to the environment

▶ how necessary the products and services they provide are

▶ how they are perceived by individuals within that environment

▶ how they are perceived by other organisations within the environment.

Difficulties often arise when organisations fail to acknowledge they are a part of that environment. By forgetting this, organisations become too insular – too consumed with their own importance. To engage successfully with their environment they need to consider themselves a small part of a much larger whole.

Environmental instability has increased in recent years due, in part, to the rapid changes societies face. This in turn has affected organisations. The likely consequences of this instability include:

► increased competition at home and overseas

► more barriers to forward planning

► more problems with changes in the external environment (such as more expensive resources, supply shortages, technological advances, strikes, improved communications, etc.)

► greater interference by government agencies at home and abroad

► greater public accountability.

To combat the problems listed above, organisations need to:

► become more flexible and adaptable
► improve their knowledge of the markets they are operating in
► become more proactive and less reactive
► improve and integrate their communication systems
► speed up their top-level decisions
► monitor and re-evaluate continuously their corporate structures
► be prepared to re-group their activities if necessary.

Organisations cannot afford to ignore the powerful external forces they encounter. Managers need to understand their external environments if their organisations are to achieve the goals they set. A first step is to distinguish between the environment's two main segments: 1) the general or 'mega' environment; and 2) the task environment.

The general or 'mega' environment

As the name implies, this refers to the overall environment within which an organisation operates. This can be further subdivided into five elements, as follows:

1. The *technological element* refers to the current state of product knowledge. This allows organisations with specialised knowledge or patents to gain at least a temporary advantage over their competitors. This drive for technological supremacy can also apply to entire countries.

2. The *economic element* refers to the production, distribution and consumption of wealth. Economic systems are a key factor here. Market forces dominate capitalist economies. In these, individuals own the means of production (directly or through corporations). Socialist economies are characterised by state ownership and control. In practice, most countries operate a mixed economy containing aspects of both capitalist and socialist systems. Within these economic systems, organisations are affected by a number of economic factors. These include inflation, interest rates, trade restrictions, tax rates, employment rates and grant availability.

3. The *legal-political element* refers to the legal and government systems that regulate the operation of organisations within their boundaries. This includes all appropriate legislation, court decisions and government regulations. Companies also have to adhere to specific laws relating to employment, health and safety, the environment and financial issues. Pressure groups representing particular interests and leading political parties also affect their operations.

4. The *sociocultural element* refers to the attitudes, values, norms, beliefs, behaviours and demographic trends of a particular country or region. This is further complicated for multinational organisations operating in various countries. Organisations need a thorough knowledge and understanding of consumers and potential consumers. This should prevent them from violating local customs or traditions. It will also help them to predict and adapt to change. Frequent and accurate monitor-

ing of trends is similarly essential for their success. This will help organisations to anticipate how people will react to existing or new products and services.

5. The *international element* affects companies who reside in or trade with different countries. In such cases, political and economic changes are largely outside their control. Political changes can range from a change of government to a military coup. Economic changes include a change in interest or exchange rates, inflation, unemployment and the imposition of trade barriers. Even organisations that do not operate outside their own national boundaries face threats from global competitors who may have plants in their countries.

Task environment
This refers to those parts of the external environment with which an organisation interacts. Major elements of the task environment are:

▶ *products and services* – it is crucial for organisations to know their main rivals, keep abreast of their developments or keep ahead of them if possible

▶ *customers and clients* – these have increasingly high expectations and a wide choice. Discovering and meeting their needs with high-quality products, services and after-sales care are essential

▶ *suppliers*, who must provide high-quality resources on demand and at competitive prices

▶ *staff*, who must be well motivated, qualified and skilled

▶ the *location(s)* from which an organisation runs its business.

To operate successfully in their environments, organisations must be able and willing to conform to appropriate cultural, social and legal requirements. These include:

▶ paying staff a competitive wage
▶ negotiating with relevant labour bodies
▶ complying with laws and government regulations.

Tutorial

Progress questions

1. Explain the difference between an organisation's internal and external environment.

2. Why is the word 'corporate' culture misleading?

3. Explain how an organisation's external environment can affect its operations.

Seminar discussion

1. Consider ways in which an organisation may successfully transmit its culture to employees at all levels.

2. Discuss how the key elements of an organisation's external environment can influence its operations.

Practical assignment

Select two large companies. Identify their corporate cultures and suggest:

▶ how these developed
▶ how well they are accepted by employees
▶ how adaptable they are to external change.

(To find this out, you may find it useful to read company handbooks and reports, to talk to employees at different levels in the organisation and to keep your eye out for reports in newspapers and on the television, etc.).

Study, revision and exam tips

1. Relate the key concepts discussed in this chapter to organisations you know.

2. Keep up to date about changes in the external environment likely to affect organisations (for example, keep your eye out for reports in the newspapers and on television and carry out searches on the Internet – particularly for government reports or summaries of these).

7

Policies and Practices

One-minute summary – Policies and procedures are the foundations upon which all organisations run their operations. Some are based on legal requirements, others on the need for good practice. In all cases the need for clarity is vital. If employees do not understand what is required of them, they cannot attain the goals set. Managers have a particularly important role to play here. It is their responsibility to help design and implement their organisation's rules and regulations. The success of an organisation depends on how effective these rules and regulations are. This chapter will help you to understand:

▶ mission statements, aims and objectives
▶ information and control systems
▶ reward systems
▶ selection and training
▶ rules, regulations and statutory requirements.

Mission statements, aims and objectives

Mission statements
An organisation's *mission* is linked to its philosophy and values. Once these are established, it is important to formalise them into a mission statement. This should incorporate the broad intentions of the organisation: its purpose – its reason for existence. These should be stated clearly but simply.

Mission statements serve a number of functions:

▶ a symbol of the organisation's philosophy
▶ a benchmark against which to measure achievements

- ▶ a declaration of purpose
- ▶ a means of establishing and developing a sense of common identity among employees
- ▶ a means for conveying an organisation's values and vision to other organisations, customers and government agencies
- ▶ a foundation on which aims and objectives, rules and regulations, and planning can be built.

Mission statements are usually shared ideas and values, and most are now provided in written form. This helps to give the organisation focus. An effective mission statement should include the following:

- ▶ a clear statement of the organisation's main products or services
- ▶ an outline of the organisation's customers
- ▶ a summary of how the organisation sees itself and of how it sees its public image
- ▶ a clear outline of the organisation's vision and plans for the future
- ▶ a clarification of the organisation's basic beliefs, philosophies and values
- ▶ a clear definition of how it will measure its success
- ▶ a dynamic statement of intent that can then be transformed into workable aims and objectives at all levels of the organisation
- ▶ a clear indication of the organisation's attitude towards its customers and employees
- ▶ an outline of how it intends to succeed.

To produce and maintain an effective mission statement, organisations need to follow a series of steps or stages. These are:

▶ conduct a SWOT analysis of the organisation

▶ appoint appropriate people to develop the mission statement

▶ collect appropriate information

▶ reach agreement on the nature and content of the mission statement

▶ produce drafts for circulation, comments and revision

▶ produce a final version of the mission statement

▶ use the mission statement to develop aims and objectives for the organisation

▶ communicate the mission statement inside and outside the organisation

▶ continuously monitor and review the mission statement.

Aims

Aims are broad statements of intent – general targets an organisation sets itself. For example, to:

▶ increase sales
▶ widen the customer base
▶ expand into new markets
▶ increase turnover
▶ move into new premises
▶ increase the number of employees.

Aims are the first stage in the development of specific directions for advancement. However, while they remain aims it is difficult to know if they have been achieved.

Objectives

Objectives are an organisation's specific goals. These should be:

▶ set out clearly
▶ precise
▶ given a timescale, if possible
▶ measurable

- ▶ achievable
- ▶ related to results.

Organisational aims can be transferred into objectives. For example, to:

- ▶ increase sales by 10% within the next twelve months
- ▶ widen the customer base by 20% within the next three years
- ▶ expand into new markets in the USA within the next four years
- ▶ increase turnover by 15% in the next twelve months
- ▶ move into new premises within five years
- ▶ increase the number of employees by approximately 800 within the next three years.

Objectives focus attention on what has to be *done*. They also help to identify strategies for success and realistic timescales. The shorter the timescales, the more precisely the objectives can be stated. Longer-term goals, on the other hand, are more likely to be revised as unexpected events occur and circumstances change.

Information and control systems

Chapter 1 introduced you to the concept of *systems*. Here we focus on two particular types of systems: information and control.

Information systems
Information systems are concerned with the complete cycle of collecting, processing, storing, retrieving and distributing information. A simple example should help to illustrate this (Figure 6). This shows how a university:

- ▶ collects data on A-level results

- ▶ transforms these into statistical analyses of subject popularity and grades

- ▶ produces a report projecting future demands for places in various departments

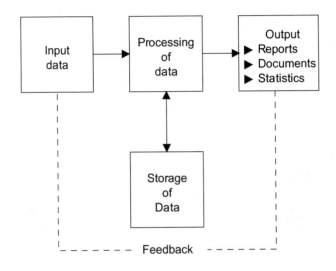

Figure 6. Basic information systems.

▶ checks the accuracy of the original data and processed results by comparing these with government forecasts for university admissions.

The example in Figure 6 demonstrates how information systems are an essential strategic and operational tool. More specifically, they aid:

▶ planning
▶ decision-making
▶ communications between different groups within the workplace
▶ communication between different grades of staff
▶ communication between the different geographical parts of an organisation
▶ effective control of all the operational elements of an

organisation
- important links with the external environment.

Not all information systems are computerised, although these certainly play a vital role in most organisations at present. Information systems do not necessarily have to be sophisticated or electronic: the type of system required depends on the nature and purpose of the information. In some instances, a simple verbal system may suffice. In others, a paper-based system may be more appropriate.

Control systems
Control systems are concerned with regulating activities within an organisation. Their aim is to make sure objectives are achieved and appropriate standards maintained. Control systems are required to regulate all aspects of an organisation's operations. More precisely, they involve regulating:

- *human resources* – to control workers' absences, punctuality, levels of productivity and quality of work produced

- *supplies* – to control their availability, cost and quality

- *equipment* – to control its efficiency, to identify problems and to organise maintenance and repairs if necessary

- *finances* – to make sure payments are made on time, time penalties are not incurred and profit margins are maintained or increased.

Control systems help managers to:

- cope with uncertainties, unforeseen problems and unpredictable elements

- detect defects, irregularities and undesirable patterns of behaviour

- identify openings for expansion, improvements to goods or services and better ways of marketing the products

- handle complex situations, such as co-ordinating effectively, seeing how different aspects of an activity fit together and overseeing projects.

Different types of control are required at various levels of the organisation:

▶ *strategic* controls are concerned with the viability of strategic plans, the availability of financial resources, adequate monitoring and information gathering

▶ *tactical* controls are concerned with monitoring results, obtaining and using feedback and taking corrective action as required

▶ *operational* controls are concerned with day-to-day monitoring, supervision and implementation, keeping to time schedules, keeping to budget and making sure employees behave appropriately.

All three types of controls are closely related. As we saw in Chapter 1, they are part of the same overall control system, or subsystems, of the main system.

Reward systems

Some form of reward system is essential if organisations are to achieve their goals. While some systems are ongoing, others are linked to specific projects or targets. The type of rewards offered will differ between organisations and with different situations.

Designing a reward system
There is no set procedure for designing an effective reward system. Points organisations need to bear in mind include:

▶ they must be fairly distributed according to productivity and the effort made
▶ they must be based on realistic, achievable targets
▶ they must be based on measurable achievements
▶ they must be sufficient to meet employee expectations

▶ they must be clearly specified

▶ they must be sufficient to motivate employees to put in effort in the future

▶ everyone must see them as fair and honest.

Types of rewards
The types of rewards offered will obviously vary according to the organisation, the job and the circumstances. Common examples include:

▶ a fixed salary or wage

▶ payment for work completed

▶ performance-related pay

▶ bonus payments based on the performance of individuals, teams or companies

▶ additional allowances for relocations or for working shifts, overtime, unsociable hours or weekends

▶ job-related perks (such as discounts on goods sold, free or cheap travel, a company car, travel expenses, pensions schemes, private health insurance, contribution towards telephone bills, luncheon vouchers or cheap loans)

▶ commission on goods or services sold

▶ fees for work done

▶ profit-sharing schemes.

Organisations can also devise special rewards systems to help them achieve particular goals (e.g. when introducing flexible working practices, job rotation or when requiring employees to work on multiple sites).

Selection and training

Both effective selection and training are essential to organisations if they are to operate effectively.

Selection

At its most simple level, selection involves matching people to jobs and is generally regarded as the activity organisations undertake when recruiting new entrants. However, selection is an ongoing process in most organisations. This happens as a result of:

▶ internal promotions
▶ movements between sections, departments, branches or divisions
▶ employees being members of different work or project teams.

Effective selection should be a two-way process: organisations decide which candidate will best meet their requirements and individuals decide if the position is the one they wish to accept. Major steps in the selection process are:

▶ *The job analysis stage.* Job tasks are identified and the skills and abilities needed to perform these jobs are matched to the tasks.

▶ *Identification of selection methods.* The best methods for selecting the right candidates are identified. These include job application forms, references, ability tests, aptitude tests, personality tests, assessment centres, graphology (the study of someone's handwriting), simulated work activities and interviews.

▶ *Implementation of selection methods.* The methods chosen are then implemented to identify the most suitable candidate for the position.

It is impossible to guarantee any selection method will provide the exact match an organisation requires. To reduce the risks of selecting the wrong candidate, organisations should make sure:

▶ the selection methods are valid: that they assess what they are designed to assess

▶ the selection methods are reliable: that they will consistently select appropriate candidates

▶ the selection is objective: based only on the selection criteria.

When *internal* applicants are involved, prior knowledge of the candidates might assist with the selection process. On the other hand, in such situations biased decisions are more likely. When *external* candidates are involved, they may prove a good match for the job but not for the organisation.

Training

Training is essential for both new entrants and for existing staff. To be effective, training should be ongoing and linked to the changing needs of staff and of the organisation. Training is usually coupled with development, although training and development have different meanings: training refers to meeting *current* needs whereas development refers to planning for *future* needs. The training process is usually divided into several phases:

1. *Carrying out a TNA* (training needs analysis). During this phase the organisation's training needs are assessed. These needs are related to the organisation's aims and objectives.

2. *Designing and implementing the training.* This involves selecting appropriate training methods and materials and organising training sessions. Training can be off-the-shelf or customised. It can be formal or informal, accredited or non-accredited. Training can be delivered by internal or external providers and on or off the premises.

3. *Evaluating the training.* This involves measuring the effectiveness of the training given.

The main types of training include the following:

▶ *Induction.* Induction is usually restricted to new entrants to the organisation but can also apply to people returning to an organisation or to those moving to new posts or grades. The key aspects covered in an induction programme relate to organisational culture, rules and regulations, procedures, task activities, colleagues, managers and the physical layout of buildings.

▶ *On the job.* This usually involves learning tasks from more highly skilled and/or experienced colleagues.

▶ *Professional updating.* This type of training usually applies to managerial and technological staff who need to keep up to date with current developments in their field.

▶ *Skills and aptitude.* This type is related to specific job requirements.

▶ *Secondments.* Secondments are usually made to other parts of the organisation to help broaden employees' knowledge and skills.

▶ *Coaching.* Employees who have difficulties with a particular area of their work are coached by a more senior member of staff to help them overcome their difficulties.

▶ *Mentoring.* Colleagues or junior members of staff are allocated a mentor who observes their work and who provides them with feedback about their performance.

▶ *Awards.* Certain members of staff may need professional qualifications to undertake their current jobs or to help their prospects of advancement.

Training has always been important, and the rapid changes that have resulted from technological advances have only served to emphasise this importance. Organisations need to keep up with, or be ahead of, their competitors. This is unlikely without a systematic, ongoing training and development programme.

Rules, regulations and statutory requirements

Together, these provide the operational framework within which organisations must work. Most organisations devise policies to cover the main areas of their operations, and these are translated into more detailed rules and regulations. Similarly, organisations must comply with a whole series of government legislation that affects their working practices.

Rules and regulations

As we saw in Chapter 2, rules and regulations tend to increase as an organisation matures and increases in size. This is because organisations need to clarify and formalise their proceedings as the workforce increases. Rules and regulations are also needed when decision-making becomes more remote and delegation more common.

For organisations to run smoothly, rules and regulations are needed in all areas of operations:

▶ *Remuneration*. Staff need guidance on when and how to submit claims for overtime, part-time hours, travel expenses, clothing allowances, queries regarding wages and salaries, the payment of bonuses and deductions.

▶ *Reporting*. The reporting of equipment breakdowns, irregularities, malpractice, accidents, absences, lateness and breaches in health and safety procedures.

▶ *Ordering*. Ordering internally from company stores or externally from outside suppliers.

▶ *Disciplinary and grievance procedures*. How to initiate these and how to proceed through to the final stages.

▶ *Notification*. Notification of holiday dates, sickness leave, compassionate leave and flexible working arrangements.

▶ *Health and safety issues*. These include bomb warnings, fire drills, evacuation of buildings, drug and alcohol abuse, smoking areas, use of equipment, dangerous work areas and prevention of accidents.

▶ *Communications*. For example, the appropriate methods of communication, the timing of communications and appropriate people for specific areas of communication.

▶ *Recruitment and dismissal*. For example, the stages to go through, the people who should be involved, employee and/ or union involvement, notice to be given, appeals procedures and feedback following job interviews.

▶ *Appraisals*. These include the preparation for and timing of appraisals, the people involved and their roles, and the regularity of appraisals.

▶ *Wage negotiations.* For example, the frequency, the people involved and conciliation and arbitration procedures.

▶ *Quality control.* These include the methods to be used, the people involved, reporting problems and seeking expert advice.

▶ *Training and development.* For example, applications for, and obtaining, finance, travel expenses and evaluation procedures.

▶ *Financial.* For example, obtaining petty cash, reimbursements, accounting systems used and times when certain financial submissions need to be made.

Statutory requirements

In many instances statutory requirements govern the rules and regulations outlined in the previous section. All the areas listed below aim to make sure organisations operate safely, and that they offer protection to their employees, customers, suppliers and to the environment:

▶ employment
▶ tax and national insurance
▶ redundancy
▶ compensation
▶ data protection
▶ consumer protection
▶ anti-discriminatory practices
▶ health and safety
▶ building regulations
▶ environmental protection
▶ industrial relations
▶ transport
▶ bankruptcy and liquidation
▶ acquisition and mergers
▶ credit.

Tutorial

Progress questions
1. Why do organisations need mission statements, aims and objectives?

2. How does the systems approach help you to understand control within organisations?

3. Why are training and development so important to organisational success?

Seminar discussion
1. Each member of the group should investigate the reward systems within an organisation of his or her choice. He or she should report back to the group and all members of the group should note the similarities and differences between the different reward systems discussed.

2. Groups should discuss the advantages and disadvantages of filling vacancies internally within organisations.

Practical assignment
Select an area of statutory requirement and investigate:

▶ how often the law has changed over the last fifty years
▶ when the law was changed
▶ what may have prompted the changes you have noted.

Study, revision and exam tips
1. Consider ways in which organisations can find loopholes in statutory requirements.

2. Link the material covered in this chapter to organisations you know.

8

Decision-Making

One-minute summary – Decision-making cannot be viewed in isolation: it needs to be considered in the context of organisational structures, culture and procedures. The pattern of decision-making within an organisation also has to be identified. Therefore we need to consider decision-making as a whole process as well as consider its component parts. Much of what is covered in this chapter should already be familiar to you as many of the key points discussed here have been dealt with elsewhere. They are brought together here, however, to help you understand:

▶ the meaning and sources of authority and power
▶ the use and misuse of authority and power
▶ organisational structures and decision-making
▶ group decision-making
▶ leadership and decision-making
▶ problems and solutions.

The meaning and sources of authority and power

All organisations need to make decisions. However, who makes these decisions, and how much authority and power these people have, differ with organisations. The main determinants of this relate to the organisation's size, structure and purpose.

The meaning and sources of authority

Authority is related to the duties and responsibilities of a particular post. These need to be defined clearly to make sure post-holders do not neglect their duties or abuse their position. Having authority entitles a person to:

- ▶ make decisions relating to his or her own level of authority
- ▶ implement decisions made at a higher level
- ▶ direct others in respect of their duties
- ▶ make sure others work towards the organisation's goals.

Authority relationships are most clearly identified in organisation charts (see Chapter 2). Charts differ, however, in how much specific information they provide: some name only posts, others only post-holders. It is usually the latter type that is the more useful because they identify key people within the organisation.

Large organisations usually need a series of charts that show the structure of their various different parts. These might include:

- ▶ offices
- ▶ branches
- ▶ sites
- ▶ departments
- ▶ sections.

People within such divisions often never meet, particularly if they are geographically distanced. However, they still need to know who has authority over what and whom to contact if the need arises.

People with authority have legitimate power and, hence, should be obeyed. People with the *same amount* of authority do not need to obey each other but they do need to respect each other's authority and reach agreement or compromise, if necessary. By setting clear lines of authority, employees know whom to obey and can legitimately refuse to accept orders from others of the same rank.

In some organisations, the authority over certain members of staff is split between managers of the same rank. This can cause confusion and difficulty for the employees involved and so, in such cases, duties and work priorities need to be clearly defined.

Some employees will have authority that is based on their level of expertise. These employees may also have direct managerial responsibilities. Alternatively, they may act in a consultative capacity to line managers. In such cases, the lines of authority may be more blurred, but they still exist.

The meaning and sources of power

We looked in some detail at power and influence in Chapter 5. Here we look at power as it relates specifically to decision-making. At first sight, authority and power may appear to be the same thing: you would expect people in authority to have power and for power to relate to the posts people hold. To some extent this is true: people with authority have the power to influence those working at lower levels. Managers generally rely on particular sources of power. These include:

▶ power based on their position within the hierarchy and the authority related to this position

▶ their ability to distribute or withhold rewards to others

▶ their ability to coerce others by way of fear of punishment for non-compliance

▶ the possession of expertise that is useful and valued

▶ the possession of important information and the option to share or conceal this

▶ their ability to make people admire, like or respect them.

However, power is not always linked to authority. As we saw in Chapter 4, some individuals exert power over others as a result of such things as:

▶ their personality characteristics
▶ the roles they play outside the organisation
▶ the relationships they have with the people who do have power
▶ possessing valuable knowledge, experience or expertise.

Power, therefore, is a very complex *human* issue and so perhaps the best way to understand it is to ask ourselves the important question:

▶ Why do people *want* power?

While the answers to this question will vary, some common replies might be:

▶ a strong desire to influence people, decisions and outcomes
▶ to enhance one's status within an organisation
▶ to enhance one's standing outside an organisation
▶ to control people and situations
▶ for the satisfaction dominating others provides
▶ to give people the opportunity to solve problems themselves
▶ to enable people to achieve their goals.

To lead effectively, therefore, managers should be aware of the main sources of unofficial power within their organisations: unofficial leaders can be dangerous if they feel alienated. As we have noted elsewhere, sensible managers will form a partnership with such leaders and will make effective use of their skills.

The use and misuse of authority and power

Use of authority and power

For an organisation to work effectively, it is important that authority and power are distributed appropriately throughout the entire organisation so that:

▶ decisions can be made at appropriate levels in the hierarchy

▶ the skills and experience of managers at all levels are used

▶ senior managers can delegate less important decision-making

▶ managers do not take unfair advantage of their position

▶ more managers feel involved in, and committed to, the decisions made.

How much authority and power is given to managers depends on the culture, objectives and structure of an organisation. Whatever its system and policy, all organisations need safeguards to prevent authority and power being misused.

Misuse of authority and power

The idea of the misuse of power can sound quite sinister and, if taken to extremes, it can be. However, in most cases, authority and power are misused for less dramatic reasons. These include:

▶ the desire to impress superiors

▶ poor decisions caused by over-anxiety

▶ unwise delegation of authority and power

▶ a lack of understanding about the parameters of authority and power

▶ weak superiors who do not monitor the managers under their control carefully

▶ managers who are over-competitive

▶ misunderstandings about rules, regulations and procedures.

Consequences of the misuse of authority and power

The misuse of authority and power, for whatever reason, can have unfortunate consequences:

▶ reduced motivation among employees
▶ fear of bullying and harassment
▶ reluctance to make decisions
▶ poor communications
▶ less effective working practices
▶ increased absenteeism
▶ increased turnover of staff.

The extent of these adverse consequences will depend on such factors as:

▶ the seniority of the manager concerned
▶ the degree of monitoring that takes place
▶ the availability of more senior managers to discuss grievances with
▶ the clarity of rules and procedures
▶ the degree and nature of the misuse.

As it is very difficult to eliminate the misuse of authority and power, it is better to prevent such problems arising in the first place. Various steps can be taken to do this:

▶ making sure duties and responsibilities are clearly set out

▶ devising an effective monitoring system

▶ making sure there is a procedure for reporting instances of misuse

▶ making sure any reported misuse is investigated and the findings acted upon

▶ safeguarding anyone reporting misuse against reprisals from the manager concerned

▶ encouraging an open, friendly atmosphere in which any problems can be discussed

▶ sharing authority and power in such a way that misuse is difficult.

Putting adequate procedures and systems in place is an important step towards reducing the misuse of authority and power but even more important is selecting the right people for managerial positions. And the more senior the position, the more the need for safeguards since the potential for misuse is greater.

Organisational structures and decision-making

As decision-making processes and the personnel involved differ with organisations, once again, the organisation chart is the first step in identifying posts and post-holders.

The pattern of decision-making within organisations

As we have noted many times, it is the senior managers who make the strategic decisions. This will involve them taking a historical perspective to the decisions that have to be made:

▶ identifying the organisation's current position

- ▶ tracking how they arrived at this position
- ▶ deciding where they want to go from there
- ▶ finding ways of reaching these goals.

While middle managers will also implement strategic decisions, they will also make less important, usually medium-term, decisions. At the lower levels, junior managers and supervisors will implement middle-management decisions and control the day-to-day running of operations.

Centralised decision-making

As we have already seen, in small organisations it is the owner who usually makes all the major decisions. The owner might also oversee routine daily operations. In larger organisations, decision-making is often hierarchical, and all authority and power will lie with senior managers. Lower-level managers will simply be responsible for the implementation of these decisions. Any decision-making powers they have will be restricted to very minor issues, and even these will have to be made within very clear guidelines and codes of practice. This type of decision-making is often referred to as 'top down'.

The main advantages of centralised decision-making are as follows:

- ▶ it is easier to co-ordinate the decisions made
- ▶ the decisions will follow the same pattern
- ▶ those making the decisions will have sufficient knowledge and experience
- ▶ senior managers have a broader perspective and are better able to balance the needs of various parts of the organisation to arrive at rational decisions
- ▶ the wasteful duplication of people, resources and time is avoided
- ▶ strong leadership is promoted.

Decentralised decision-making

Some organisations prefer to decentralise their decision-making. This is most likely to occur when:

▶ an organisation grows too large for centralised decisions

▶ parts of the organisation are widely dispersed geographically

▶ rapid change means decision-makers have to be in constant touch with events in the outside environment

▶ rapid change makes it difficult for senior managers to keep up to date with all aspects of the organisation (e.g. technical, product and market information)

▶ senior managers find it difficult to keep up to date with advances in technology

▶ advances in technology make it easy for managers in different locations to keep in close contact with each other and with head office.

Some organisations prefer to involve their staff, at all levels, in the decision-making process. This may be through committees containing representatives of staff from different sections and levels. Alternatively, staff may be encouraged to make suggestions for improving any aspect of the business. In such cases, the organisational structure needs to allow for the flow of information and suggestions up from the bottom to the top. The name 'bottom up' is often used to describe this process.

Group decision-making

Decisions made by groups of people are probably the most common types of decisions found in organisations. These decisions can be made by such groups as permanent work teams, temporary project teams and boards of directors, etc.

The advantages of group decisions

The popularity of group decision-making is based on a number of factors. These include:

▶ the pooling of information, knowledge, skills, expertise and experience

▶ the opportunity for individuals to bounce ideas off each other

▶ the tendency for groups to be better at problem-solving than individuals

▶ there is shared responsibility for the decisions made

▶ a greater sense of commitment to the decisions made

▶ a greater understanding of the decisions made

▶ opportunities for group members to develop decision-making skills.

Disadvantages of group decisions

Group decisions are not always appropriate or the best solution. In some instances, the need for security or specialist knowledge make it essential an individual makes the decisions. It will also depend on whether the organisation favours involving its employees in its decision-making processes in the first place.

The disadvantages of group decisions include:

▶ groups may find it difficult to reach an agreement

▶ group decisions may cause conflict between group members

▶ some decisions are too complex for group involvement

▶ dominant group members may over-ride the views of others

▶ groups usually take longer to reach decisions

▶ groups may be too inclined to reach a consensus rather than the best possible solution.

However, the use of small groups, careful planning and the selection of the right team members should lessen the impact of these disadvantages.

Leadership and decision-making

We identified the need for effective leadership in Chapter 4. Making decisions is an important part of a leader's role, and earlier in this chapter we saw that the type of decisions made will depend largely on an individual's position in the organisation's hierarchy.

Senior managers and decision-making

As we noted earlier, senior managers are responsible for strategic decisions. To make these decisions they need to:

▶ have a thorough knowledge of the organisation's position in the marketplace

▶ know the organisation's main competitors

▶ be aware of external factors likely to affect their organisation's success

▶ link their decisions to the organisation's mission statement and goals

▶ know the options available and their likely consequences.

To be effective, strategic plans need to be:

▶ innovative
▶ flexible
▶ responsive to the needs of key parties
▶ realistic
▶ clear and easy to understand.

While senior managers have overall leadership responsibility for strategic decisions, they will also have to delegate some decision-making responsibilities to other members of their organisations.

Effective delegation

Delegation is concerned with giving others appropriate authority and responsibility to carry out specific tasks or to take over certain operations from someone more senior. Managers at all levels have important leadership roles to play, and part of this role is to act as a filter when passing decisions from the top down to the workforce. They are also responsible for channelling ideas upwards from individuals and teams.

Senior managers usually delegate certain types of decisions to middle managers. This may involve devising innovative ways to implement higher-level strategic decisions. Alternatively, it may require obtaining ideas from people who are in a better position to know exactly what is needed.

Delegation can also occur at lower levels. For example, individuals or team leaders can be given responsibility for particular projects or tasks. This has the advantage of:

▶ preparing people for more responsible jobs
▶ taking advantage of a wide range of skills, expertise and experience
▶ increasing staff motivation
▶ involving more people in decision-making
▶ increasing levels of commitment to the decisions made.

Effective delegation will only work if an organisation's structure and culture are geared towards this. It is also important to establish clear boundaries of responsibility, to monitor progress and to provide the necessary support.

Problems and solutions

No matter how carefully something is planned, problems can occur. When this happens, solutions must be found.

Problems
A simple way of viewing a problem is as something that should not be happening, and problems almost inevitably result from a change or deviation from whatever is normal in a particular situation. Problems, therefore, are a regular occurrence in any decision-making process.

When things do go wrong it is imperative to:

▶ recognise there is a problem
▶ define the problem clearly
▶ diagnose the source of the problem.

Solutions

Simply knowing there is a problem isn't enough: we need to find solutions. Unfortunately there are rarely ready-made solutions to all the problems encountered. Hence, we need to investigate the nature of the problem to find its cause. Once the cause has been established, we then need to set up and test a number of hypotheses to solve the problem. This involves posing and trying to answer a series of questions. The exact questions asked will depend on the situation. However, as a general guide they should include the following:

▶ What happened?
▶ When did it happen?
▶ Why did it happen?
▶ Who was involved?

When posing and answering questions like these, it is useful to *reverse* the situation. For example, instead of asking why something *did* happen, ask why it did *not* happen. Ask what would happen if I did *not* do this, as well as what would happen if I *did*. It is also useful to employ the following procedure:

▶ keep referring questions and answers back to the original cause

▶ check how each alternative solution can address the problem identified

▶ consider the short, medium and long-term effects of solutions

▶ continuously monitor progress when testing options

▶ when a solution is agreed, keep on monitoring to assess the consequences.

While we cannot prevent problems from arising, we can be ready for them when they do occur. Knowing what to do is *useful*; taking appropriate action is *essential*.

Tutorial

Progress questions
1. What are the main sources of authority within a large organisation?

2. How can power be misused?

3. How effective is group decision-making?

Seminar discussion
1. How can organisations safeguard against the misuse of power?

2. How can effective delegation aid decision-making?

Practical assignment
Identify a major decision made within the last twelve months by an organisation known to you:

▶ What led to this decision being made?
▶ What problems arose when implementing the decision?
▶ How were these problems resolved?
▶ How could these problems have been avoided?

Study, revision and exam tips
1. Avoid considering the issues raised in this chapter in the abstract. Wherever possible, make sure you link them to actual situations.

2. Since most of the issues raised in this chapter relate to other chapters in the book, try to link issues to test your understanding of them.

9

Development and Change

One-minute summary – To thrive in an increasingly competitive environment, organisations must constantly adapt and develop. An organisation's ability to change effectively will be closely related to its culture, structure and style of leadership. It can also learn from its past experiences. Organisations often face common problems. Because of this, they can also learn from the experience of others, which may prevent them from making similar costly mistakes. Whatever the reasons for change, the full implications of the change must be considered. Equally important, the full consequences of not changing should also be reviewed. This chapter will help you to understand:

▶ dynamic organisations
▶ learning organisations
▶ the need and pressure for change
▶ the processes of change
▶ the barriers to change
▶ the implications of change and non-change
▶ organisations of the future.

Dynamic organisations

Dynamism conjures up visions of energy, enthusiasm and drive. If we apply this concept to organisations, a dynamic organisation will be one that is seen to be thrusting and competitive and ready to accept change. However, this view of a dynamic organisation should be treated with caution. Organisational change cannot be considered in isolation: it must be linked to other factors already covered in this book, such as the organisation's:

▶ structure
▶ culture
▶ leadership styles
▶ position within the marketplace
▶ vision
▶ stability
▶ external environment.

Previous chapters have stressed the importance of striking a healthy balance between change and stability. These, in turn, are related to the speed of change taking place and the organisation's ability to cope with this rate of change. An important part of this ability is the organisation's desire to learn from internal and external experiences.

Learning organisations

Do organisations learn *themselves* or is it more a case of the *people* within the organisation learning?

Learning by individuals

In Chapter 7 we discussed the importance of training and development. This importance has long been recognised by both employers and the government but training and development still do not always receive the priority they deserve. However, the current emphasis on 'lifelong learning' and the 'learning age' serve to reinforce the importance of learning.

It is the individuals within organisations who learn. It is their knowledge and skills that enable an organisation to prosper. If we accept this, what role does the organisation play in individual learning? Organisations need to:

▶ create an atmosphere conducive to learning

▶ make full use of the knowledge and skills of their employees at all levels

▶ build a learning community by providing a sense of cohesion

▶ encourage ongoing learning. This relates both to individuals currently employed by the organisation and to individuals entering and leaving the organisation.

Organisations have an important role to play in learning although having a training and development policy and plan is not sufficient: they need to play a more strategic role. Key factors in this are providing a sense of:

▶ cohesion
▶ identity
▶ continuity.

If co-ordinated wisely, individual learning in an organisation will result in something more than an aggregate of knowledge and skills: it will provide a learning organisation. An organisation that is aware of:

▶ what is required
▶ how to achieve this
▶ the consequences of achieving particular goals
▶ the consequences of not achieving particular goals.

The company itself must learn, as well as the individuals that comprise the company.

The learning organisation

Organisations constantly acquire, process and use knowledge. This helps them to:

▶ know what is happening in the marketplace
▶ make effective predictions
▶ anticipate relevant economic, legal, political, social and technological changes.

How organisations respond to this knowledge will depend on how well they know themselves and their needs. An important part of learning, therefore, is organisations knowing what suits them best.

This is crucial if they are to rise to challenges and keep ahead of their competitors.

Organisations learn in various ways:

▶ collecting and processing data from within the organisation and from their external environment

▶ by trial and error

▶ from observation of other organisations

▶ from past experiences – both from within and from outside their own boundaries.

The importance of managing information should not be under-estimated, and the way information is managed must allow organisations to transfer what they know to different situations and circumstances. In other words, it should enable them to be adaptable and flexible.

The need and pressure for change

Change involves some form of alteration to an organisation's status quo: organisations become different in some way. Hence change is not the same as innovation – innovation involves a new initiative that is in some way related to an organisation's processes, products or services. In other words, while innovation always implies change, not all change is innovative.

The need for change

Many organisations suffer from inertia: they prefer what is comfortable and familiar and are reluctant to change unless this becomes necessary. However, the need for change may result from forces outside the organisation's control, and *reactive* change of this kind is far from ideal. It implies a crisis, which could threaten an organisation's existence.

Alternatively, organisations may have recognised the need for change and have planned for this. Planned change, therefore, has been more carefully considered and implies foresight and vision.

Pressures for change

As we have already seen, pressures for change can arise from both internal and external sources. Examples of *internal* sources include:

- ▶ high production costs
- ▶ high staff turnover
- ▶ high staff absenteeism
- ▶ a high number of grievances
- ▶ strikes
- ▶ difficulties in reaching decisions
- ▶ site changes
- ▶ restructuring
- ▶ rationalisation
- ▶ redundancies
- ▶ the stage reached in the organisation's life-cycle.

Some of these, such as strikes, rationalisation and restructuring, are fairly clear pressures for change. Others, such as high staff turnover, absenteeism and difficulties in making decisions, are much more subtle pressures.

External pressures for change are often outside an organisation's control. These may be classified as economic, political, social and technological changes. For example:

- ▶ changes in demand for products or services
- ▶ a change in legislation
- ▶ a change in the age distribution among the population
- ▶ a change in the rate of inflation, exchange rates or unemployment
- ▶ a change of government
- ▶ supply difficulties
- ▶ a change in the number of young people staying on in further or higher education
- ▶ expanding or contracting markets for products or services
- ▶ changes in consumer tastes and fashions
- ▶ technological changes.

The processes of change

Change is usually not sudden: it involves a series of processes or steps that ultimately bring about the desired (or undesired) transformation.

The stages of change

Change – even rapid change – usually goes through this series of phases or stages. The exact number of these stages may vary, but key stages include the following:

▶ recognising there is a need for change. This may be associated with an internal or external problem. Alternatively, it may be in response to an opportunity to improve operations or to expand market share

▶ identifying or diagnosing the problem or opportunity. This is usually followed by the generation of ideas about how to react to what has been found

▶ it may then be necessary to present proposals for change to the appropriate people

▶ identifying potential barriers to any proposals made and how to overcome these

▶ taking appropriate action to implement the proposed changes

▶ monitoring and evaluating the effects of any changes implemented. If adjustments are required, these should be made.

The components of change

There are several key components that need to be considered when planning or implementing change. These have all been discussed elsewhere in this book, and their reappearance here highlights the importance of the systems approach in demonstrating how these components fit together.

▶ An organisation's *structure* provides the framework within which change will take place. This includes the leadership hierarchy, departmental divisions and the communication system. It is the nature of these that will determine how change is managed.

► The *human resources* employed by an organisation are crucial to successful change. It is people's commitment, expertise and skills that enable plans to be made and implemented.

► The *technology* used by organisations provides the knowledge, equipment and tools necessary to accomplish change.

► An organisation's *culture* supplies the conditions conducive to change. Shared beliefs, values and vision help to determine the direction of change an organisation takes.

If we consider the components of change separately, we will be able to understand the nature and mechanisms of change. However, to manage change successfully, we need to understand the *relationships* between these various components.

The barriers to change

In most organisations there will be, quite naturally, some resistance to change. To manage change effectively, organisations need to anticipate this resistance and to overcome the obstacles to change.

Reasons for resistance
Both individuals and groups are likely to resist change. However, we need to distinguish between those who resist all forms of change and those who are more selective. In both instances, the reasons for resistance might include:

► fear of the unknown
► being comfortable with the current situation
► having insufficient information about the change
► not understanding what is going to happen
► being influenced by others who dislike the idea of change

► feeling discriminated against
► feeling threatened by the proposed changes.

In some instances such fears will be justified. In others, consulting those affected by the change and good systems of communication usually reduce resistance.

Resistance tactics
The resistance tactics people adapt will vary according to the type and extent of change, the strength of the support they receive and the chances of their resistance succeeding. Common tactics include:

► refusing to implement change
► sabotage
► taking industrial action
► seeking support from shareholders
► seeking support from people in a position of power
► searching for evidence to prove that change is unnecessary or undesirable.

Organisational obstacles to change
Sometimes obstacles to change can originate within the organisation itself rather than in its employees. Examples include:

► an unwillingness or inability by senior management to recognise the need for change

► difficulties caused by the upheavals the change will involve (e.g. the introduction of new technology, changing work patterns and relocations)

► structural problems (e.g. if the change involves merger or acquisition)

► deciding when to change successful operating practices (there is a danger of waiting until problems arise rather than anticipating a need for change)

► a reluctance to expand into new geographical markets

▶ a reluctance to develop new products or services.

In addition to internal obstacles, organisations also face external obstacles to change. These are usually associated with:

▶ changes in the wider economy (e.g. higher inflation or interest rates)

▶ changes in international trade (e.g. unfavourable exchange rates)

▶ competitors gaining a larger share of the market

▶ problems with supplies

▶ a change of government policy (e.g. reduced aid for relocating to deprived areas).

The implications of change and non-change

The implications of change
The motive for change is usually improvement – to operations, industrial relations, market share or profits. However, the consequences of change are sometimes difficult to predict accurately. In some cases, the improvement may be immediate and long lasting. In others, they may occur quite swiftly but not be last long. In some situations, the change may even worsen an organisation's position.

Successful change, therefore, generally reflects the amount of research and planning the organisation has undertaken, but unforeseen circumstances can disrupt even the most careful of plans.

The implications of non-change
Whenever change is planned, organisations must ask themselves the following questions:

▶ Is the change required to solve a particular problem?
▶ Is the change required to improve overall operational efficiency?

▶ Is the change required in response to external changes?
▶ Is the change required to take advantage of opportunities?

In each case, organisations must also ask themselves the following, *additional* question:

▶ What will happen if the change does not take place?

If the answer to this question suggests the company's survival will be at risk, then change appears inevitable. However, if the change appears desirable rather than essential, the options for change should be considered.

There are several reasons why change does not take place. These include:

▶ the costs are too high

▶ there is insufficient support for the change

▶ the decision to change is outside the organisation's hands. This may occur if a merger or acquisition does not go ahead or planning permission is not granted

▶ circumstances may overtake the schedule for change, making the proposed change too difficult or unnecessary.

Organisations of the future

It is impossible to predict accurately what organisations will be like in the future. However, present trends do suggest some potentially interesting changes. The extent to which these changes occur will depend on:

▶ the nature of an organisation
▶ technological advances
▶ government legislation
▶ economic and social developments.

Given these restrictions, developments in the following areas seem likely:

▶ ethics is likely to assume a more prominent position

▶ technological advances will increase and become more widespread

▶ there will be tighter controls (e.g. in relation to data protection, pollution safeguards and general accountability)

▶ more effective systems of communication will become increasingly important

▶ there will be a greater balance between employees' working lives and their home lives

▶ more flexible working arrangements in relation to hours worked and the place of work

▶ employees will become more valued and better protected

▶ employees will have greater expectations of work and will be more prepared to put pressure on employers to fulfil their obligations

▶ the age distribution of the workforce will continue to be biased in favour of older workers

▶ the trend towards a multi-skilled workforce will continue

▶ there will be a greater emphasis on the global marketplace

▶ a greater understanding of other cultures will be needed

▶ a more flexible retirement policy will operate

▶ there will be a further growth of jobs in the service sector.

Some organisations are better prepared to respond to these changes than others, and these are the ones that are most likely to succeed in the future.

Tutorial

Progress questions
1. Why is it important for employees to engage in lifelong learning?

2. What is meant by the term 'learning organisation'?

3. Why is change inevitable for organisations?

Seminar discussion

1. How can you have change without innovation?

2. What are the main barriers to change within the transport industry?

Practical assignment

Identify a major change that has taken place in the banking industry within the last five years. Discuss:

▶ why this change occurred;
▶ the main implications for the change for staff and customers.

Study, revision and exam tips

1. Consider development and change in relation to other parts of the syllabus.

2. Consider development and change in relation to any organisation in which you have worked or of which you have some knowledge.

Glossary

This glossary is intended as a guide to help you understand some of the key words used in the book. It is divided into chapter headings, although some words appear in more than one chapter. Where this happens, explanations are not duplicated.

Chapter 1: Organisations as systems

biological systems Living, self-maintaining systems.

closed system A self-contained, self-sufficient system. One that is cut off from the outside world.

complex Intricate; comprising two or more parts.

environment What lies outside a boundary. External conditions that affect what occurs inside a boundary.

macro To take a broad approach; an overview.

mechanical systems Referring to various types of machine. Once set in motion the processes continue in a cyclical manner without outside interference.

micro Viewed from the perspective of small parts; these may reflect or represent the whole.

open system A system that interacts with its environment; it influences, and is influenced by, its environment.

organisations Formalised groups of people engaged in common, goal-directed activities within specified boundaries.

simple Clear, intelligible, plain.

social systems Relating to society.

subsystems Smaller groupings, often operating as systems, within the system as a whole. Parts or areas of a system.

systems A set of inter-related parts or components that together form a whole.

Chapter 2: Organisational structure and design

authority The right to make decisions, to implement decisions and to direct others.

bureaucratic Formal; relies on rules, regulations, policies and procedures; rational; rigid.

design To draw an outline of; to plan; to calculate.

dual pressure Equal pressure from different sources.

external Outside the boundaries of an organisation.

functional Having a special purpose.

horizontal On the same level.

hybrid Not pure; a combination of different types.

in-depth competence Becomes standardised.

internal Within an organisation.

matrix A system that allows functional and product structures to be used together.

organic Flexible; can respond quickly and efficiently.

organisation chart A visible representation of the underlying activities and processes within an organisation.

structure The formal pattern of interactions and co-ordination that enables an organisation to operate.

technology Transformation processes; how an organisation changes its inputs into outputs.

vertical Upright; lines of authority.

Chapter 3: Technological and environmental issues

automation The use of machines to assist or replace people who are working in organisations.

CIM (Computer-integrated manufacturing) A combination of task mechanisation and computerised information processing as used in manufacturing.

complex environment An environment where a lot of things are happening.

customised Manufactured to meet specific needs and requirements.

expert systems Computer programs modelled on the thought processes of experts in a particular field that can make decisions and solve problems.

gold collar Workers with high-level business management and technological skills.

mass produced Large-scale production of standardised products.

mechanisation Machines programmed to carry out tasks more quickly, more precisely and more conscientiously than human workers.

munificence Liberality; generosity.

robot A machine programmed to perform complex functions in a similar way to humans.

Chapter 4: Individuals

attitudes A relatively stable set of interest, opinions or purposes; expecting a certain type of experience.

expectations Anticipation; looking forward to; the prospect of.

leadership To exercise authority; to exert influence so goals may be achieved.

learning To acquire knowledge or skills; to change our behaviour as a result of experience.

motivation What directs our behaviour; makes us do things.

perception Interpretation of (giving meaning to) information received from our environment.

psychological contract The expectations employers and employees have of each other.

values A measure or standard; an estimation of worth.

Chapter 5: Groups

conflict To clash, oppose, disagree with.

dynamics A force in motion; functional; driving energy.

groups Two or more individuals working together towards some common goals or purpose.

influence Helps to determining our behaviour.

power Authority over others; capacity for action.

teams Temporary or permanent task groups.

team-building Ways of helping groups to work together effectively.

Chapter 6: Culture and the external environment

corporate A legally united body, such as a company.

culture A collection of shared attitudes, beliefs, values, norms, rituals, laws and norms.

mega The largest; overall.

structure A way of building, of constructing; a framework; an arrangement of parts.

subculture Part or division within a wider culture.

task Allocation of work; specific duties.

Chapter 7: Policies and practices

aims Broad statements of intent; targets to be achieved.

control systems Ways of regulating activities.

mission statement A statement of philosophy, values and intentions.

objectives The specific, measurable goals of an organisation.

regulations Rules, method of control, enforcing; keeping in order.

reward systems Recompense for physical or mental labour.

rules Directive; prescriptive; something that must be obeyed.

selection To pick out; to choose.

statutory A legal requirement.

training The process of instruction and development.

Chapter 8: Decision-making

authority Legal power or right linked to a post or office.

centralisation Decision-making and co-ordination rest with one or a few individuals.

decentralisation Delegation of authority and power to lower levels.

decision-making The process of making decisions.

problem Something difficult to work out.

solution Finding answers to problems.

Chapter 9: Development and change

barriers Obstacles or obstructions; limits or boundaries.

change To alter; to make different; to shift stance or position.

component A constituent part.

need To require or want; a necessity.

pressure Demanding; exerting influence.

processes Transformation; a series of actions that implement a change.

resistance Opposition or hindrance.

stages A degree of progress; a step or point of development.

Further Reading

Bartol, K M and Martin, D C (1991) *Management*. McGraw-Hill, New York.

Clegg, C W *et al*. (1985) *Case Studies in Organisational Behaviour*. Harper & Row, London.

Daft, R (1989) *Organisation Theory and Design*. West Publishing, St Paul, MN.

Dalton, G W and Lawrence, P R (eds) (1970) *Organisational Structure and Design*. Irwin-Dorsey, Chicago, IL.

Eyre, E C and Pettinger, R (1999) *Mastering Basic Management*. Macmillan, London.

Gowler, D *et al*. (1993) *Case Studies in Organisational Behaviour and Human Resource Management*. Paul Chapman Publishing, London.

Handy, C (1976) *Understanding Organisations*. Penguin Education, Harmondsworth.

Heald, G (1970) *Approaches to the Study of Organisational Behaviour: Operational Research and Behavioural Science*. Tavistock, London.

Kast, F E and Rasenzweig, J E (1970) *Organization and Management: A Systems and Contingency Approach*. McGraw-Hill Kogakusha, Tokyo.

Khandwalla, P N (1998) *Design of Organizations*. Harcourt Brace Jovanovich International Edition, New York.

Northcraft, G B and Neal, M A (1990) *Organisational Behavior: A Management Challenge*. Dryden Press, Chicago, IL.

Nystrom, P C and Starbuck, W H (1988) *Handbook of Organisational Design*. Oxford University Press, Oxford.

Robbins, S P (ed) (1986) *Organizational Behavior: Concepts, Controversies, and Applications*. Prentice-Hall, Englewood Cliffs, NJ.

Robbins, S P (1990) *Organization Theory: Structure, Design, and Application*. Prentice-Hall, Englewood Cliffs, NJ.

Wieland, G F and Ullrich, R A (1976) *Organizational Behavior, Design and Change*. Irwin, Homewood, IL.

Web sites

Miscellaneous
Blackwells Publications
http://www.blackwellpublishers.co.uk

British Export Directory
www.britishexports.com

British Psychological Society
www.bps.org.uk

Creativity Unleashed (free information)
www.cul.co.uk (software, bookshop and links)

Department of Trade and Industry
www.dti.gov.uk

Directed Creativity (various information)
www.directedcreativity.com

Financial statistics
http://www.ons.gov.uk

GEC (General Electric Co.) Revisions
http://www.gec.com

Institute of Management
http://www.inst-mgt.org.uk

Chartered Institute of Personnel and Development
www.ipd.co.uk

Lucia's Creativity Links
(eclectic set of links to various sites)

www.waterw.com/-lucia/awlinks.html

Marketing Handbook
http://www.fifi.co.uk

Journals

Chemistry and Industry
www.bio-innovations.co.uk

Chemistry in Britain
http://www.rsc.org

Chemtech
http://pubs.ass.org

Clean Air and Environmental Protection
http://www.3.mistral.co.uk/cleanair

Cross-Link (Journal of Rapra Technology)
http://www.rapra.net

Discover
www.discover.com

Economic Quarterly
http://www.rich.frb.org.ec

Export (Journal of the Institute of Export)
www.export.org.uk

Export Digest
www.croner.co.uk

Food Marketing and Manufacturing
www.urschel.com

Going US
www.outbound.newspapers.com

Harvard Business Review
http://www.hbr.org/forum (author/reader forum)

Harvard Business Review
http://www.hbsp.harvard.educ (for article reprints)

Health and Safety
http://www.open.gov.uk/hse/hsehome.html

Health and Safety Practitioner
http://www.iosh.co.uk

Henley Manager Update
www.braybrooke.co.uk

Industrial and Labour Relations Review
http://www.ilr.cornell.educ/depts/ll.Rrev

Management Decision
http://www.mcb.co.uk

Management Today
http://www.bestpractice.haynet.com

People Management
www.peoplemanagement.co.uk

Professional Manager
www.deltaweb.co.uk/nelc

The Service Industries Journal
http://www.frankcass.com

Society of Business Economists/The Business Economist Journal
www.sbe.co.uk

World of Work
http://www.ilo.org.uk

Index